Royal
Coloring Book

Aryla Publishing 2020

978-1-912675-92-0

www.arylapublishing.com

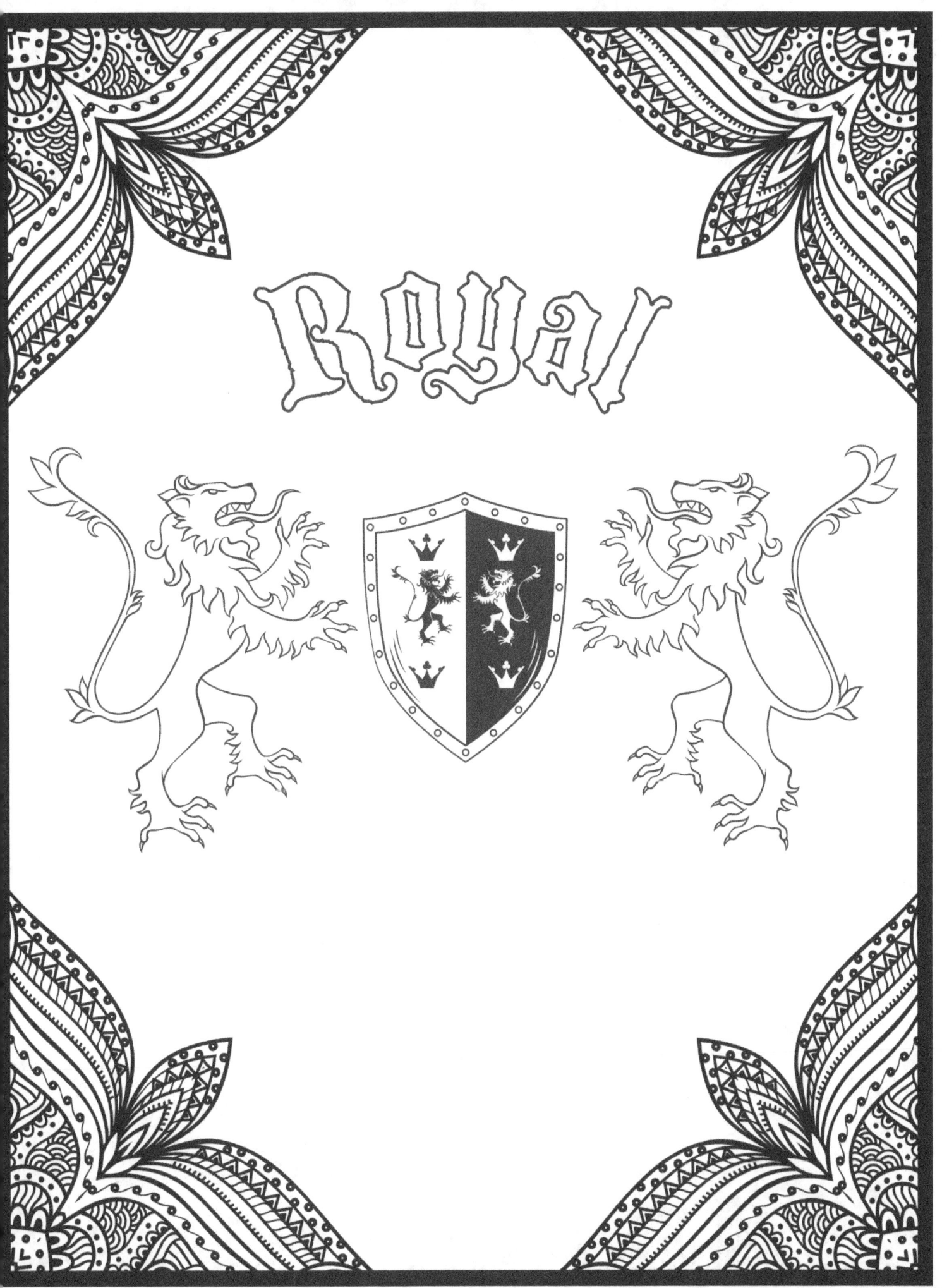

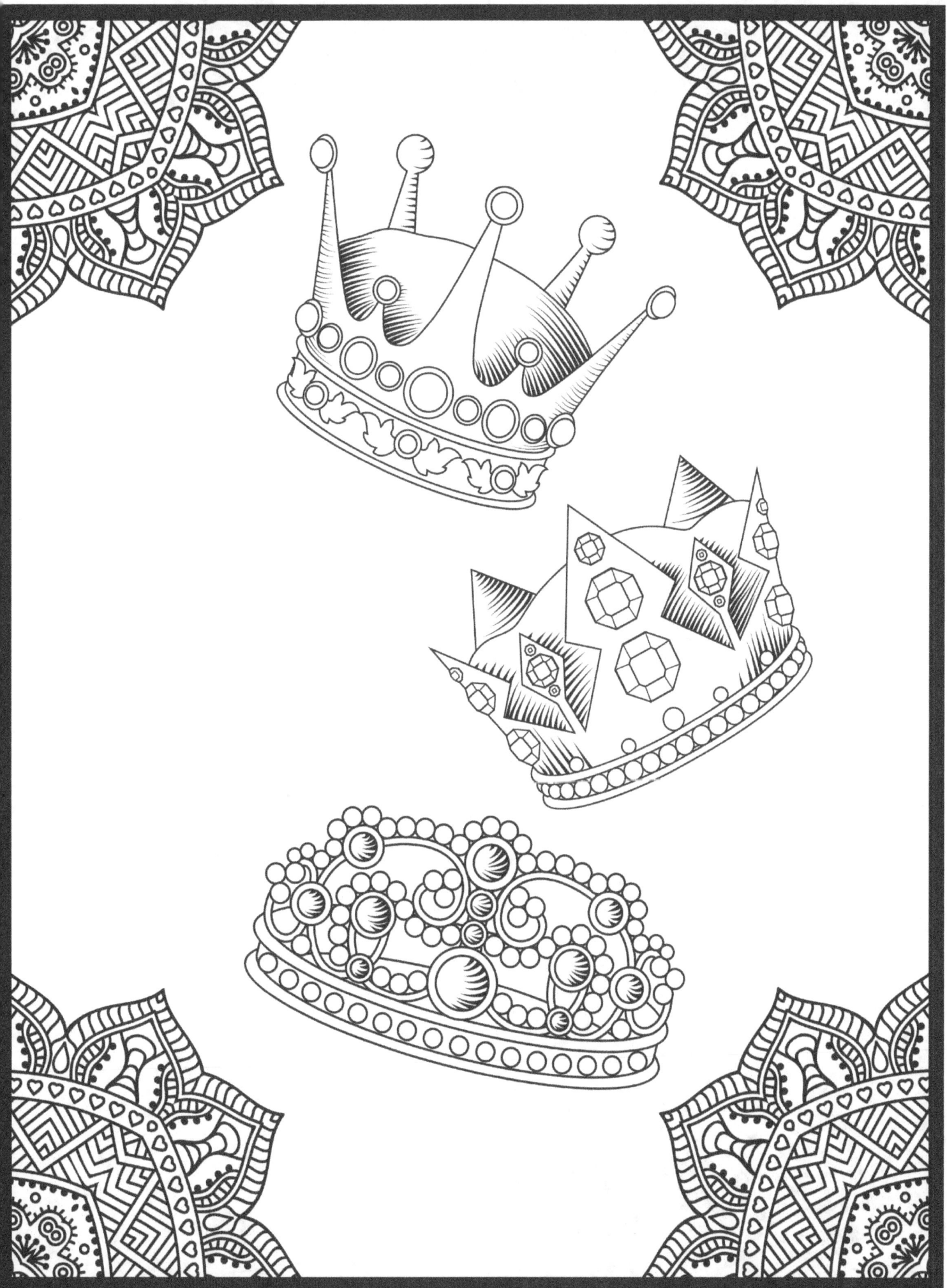

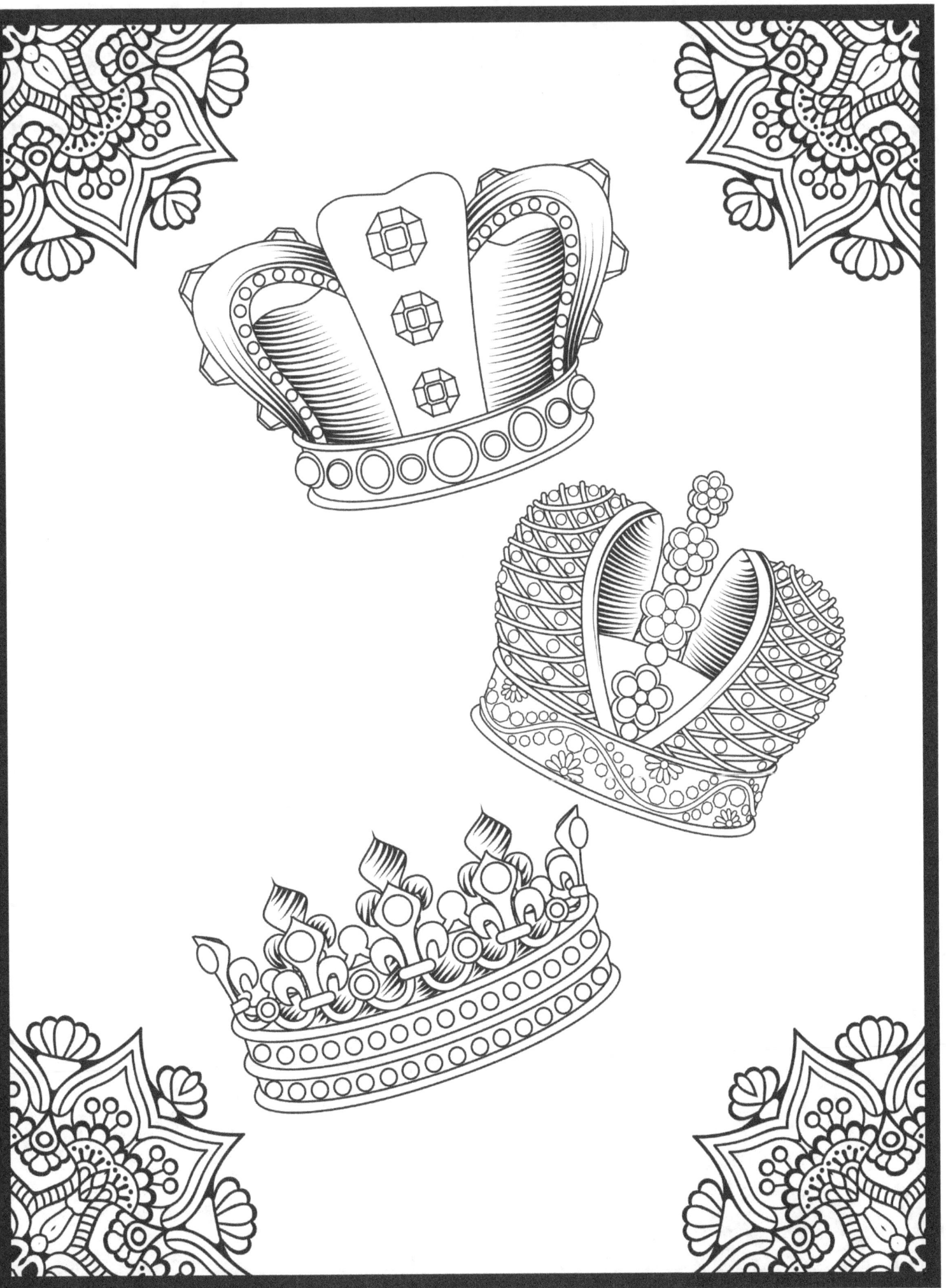

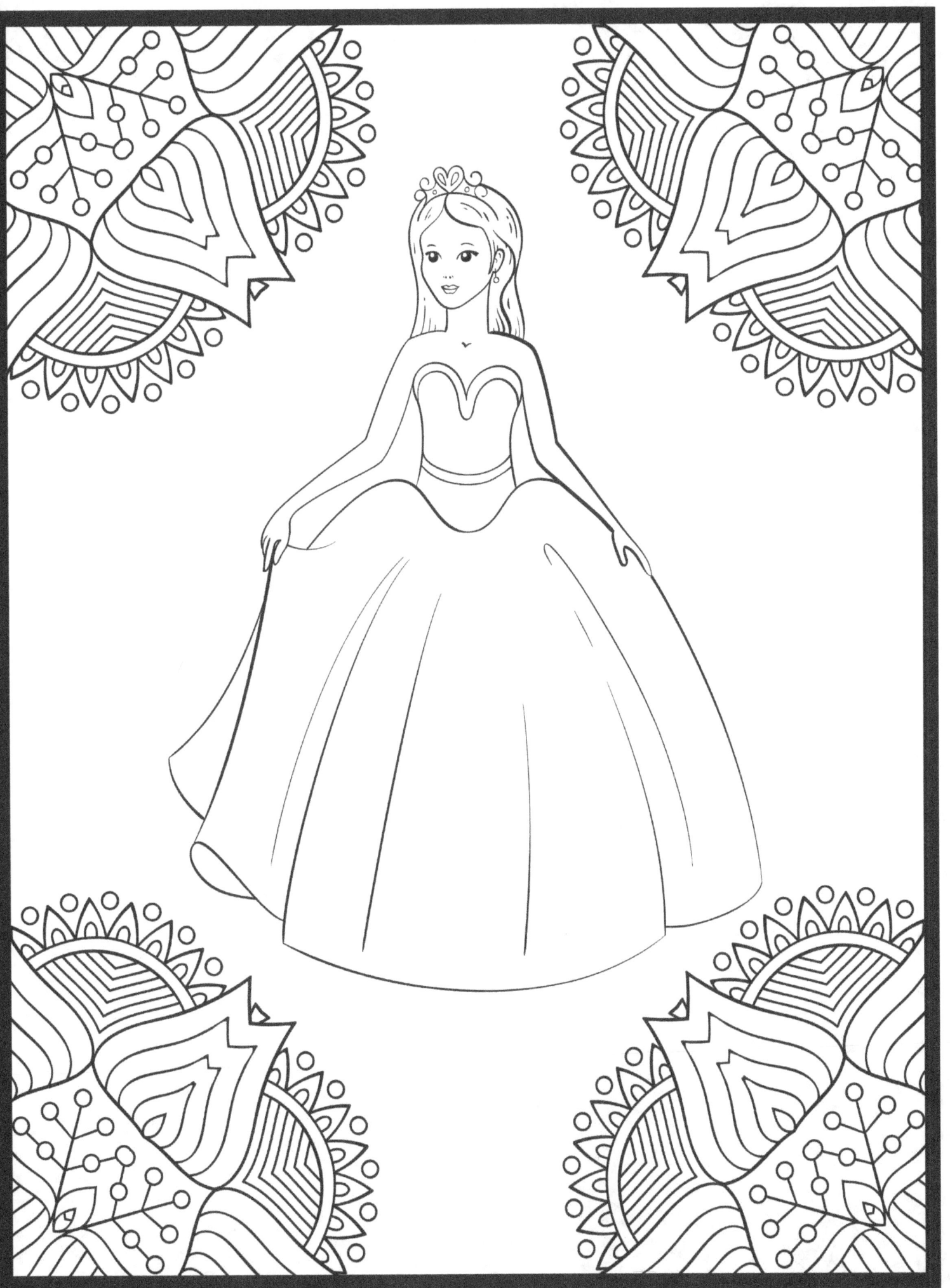

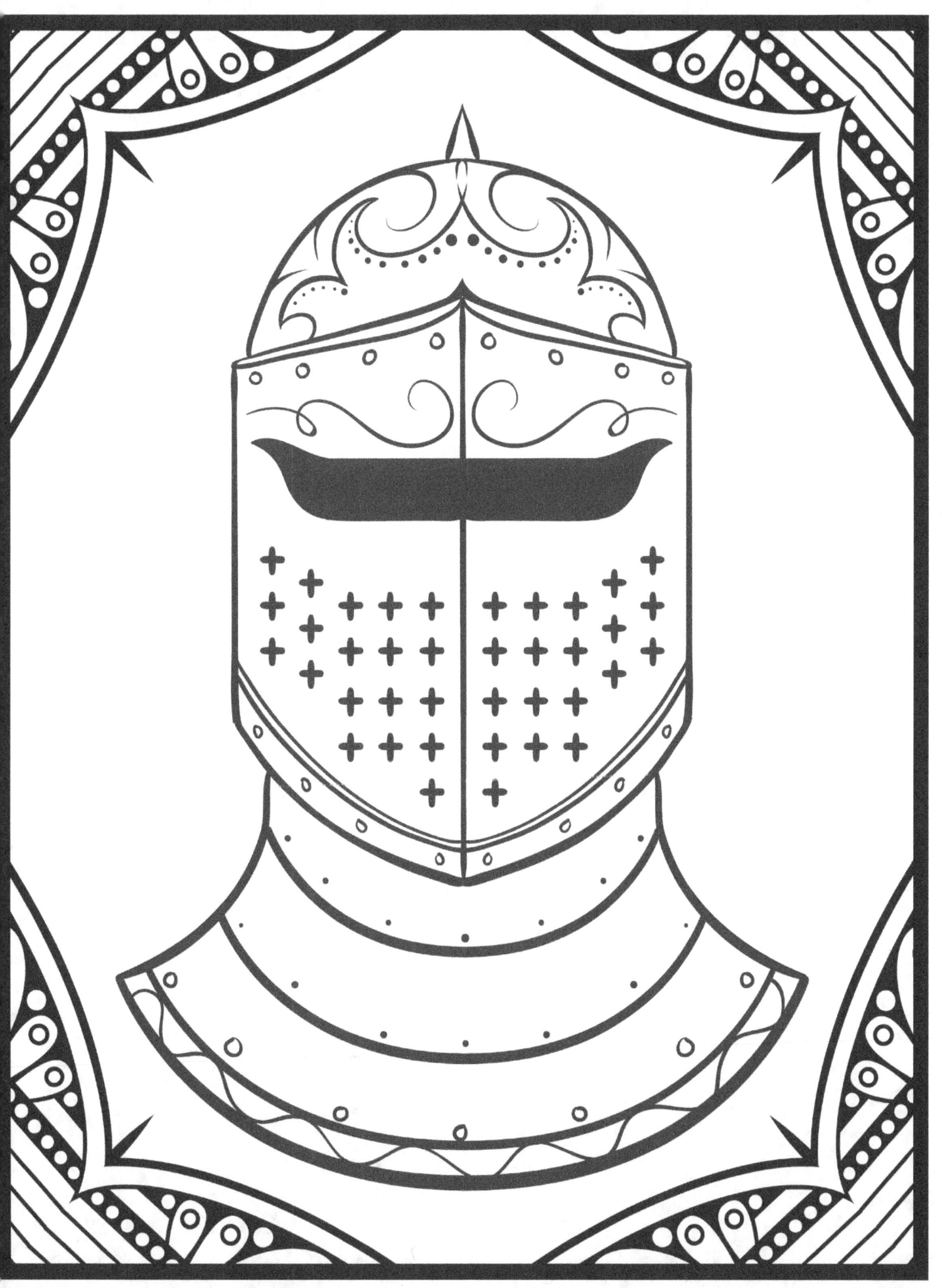

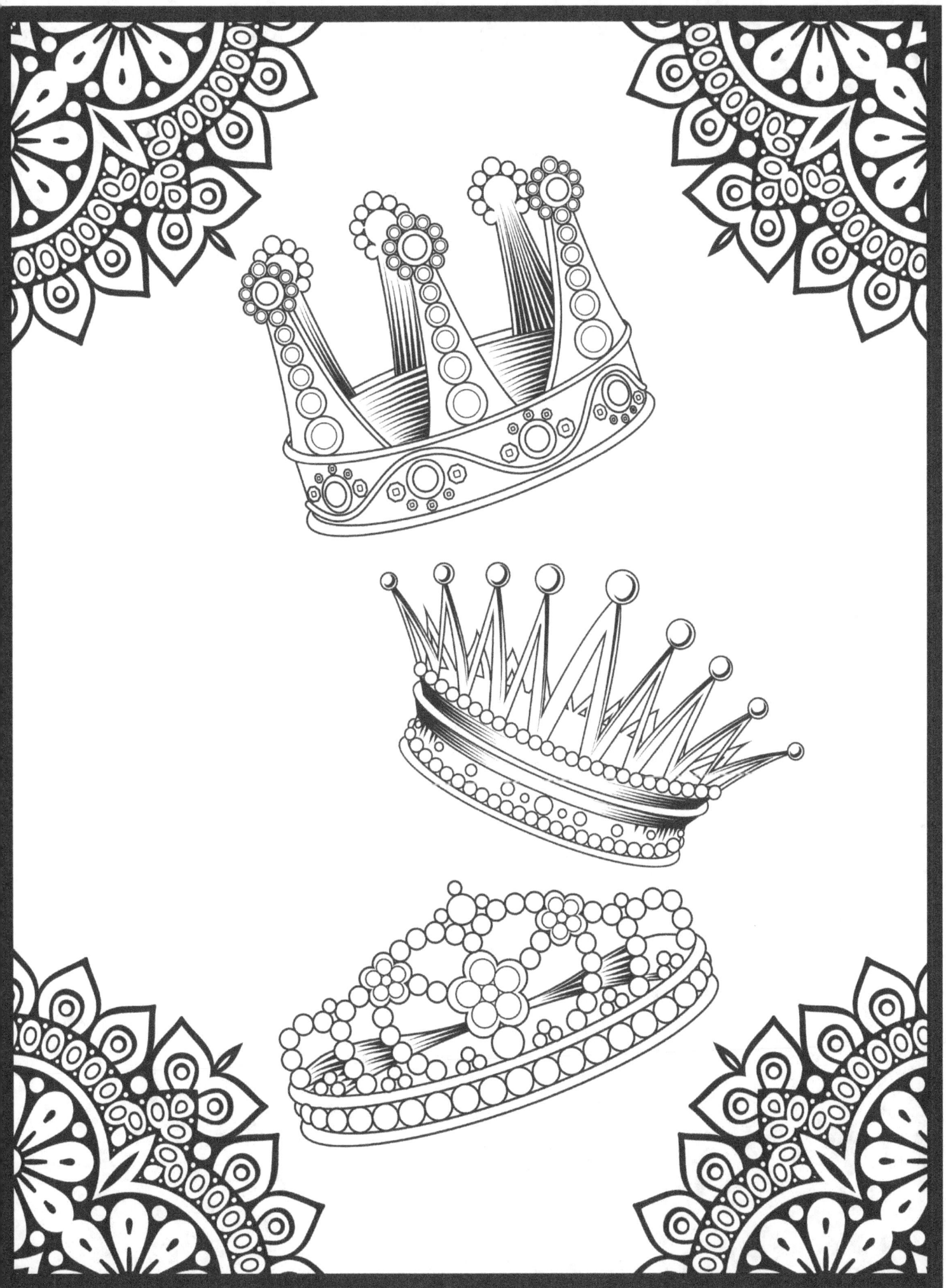

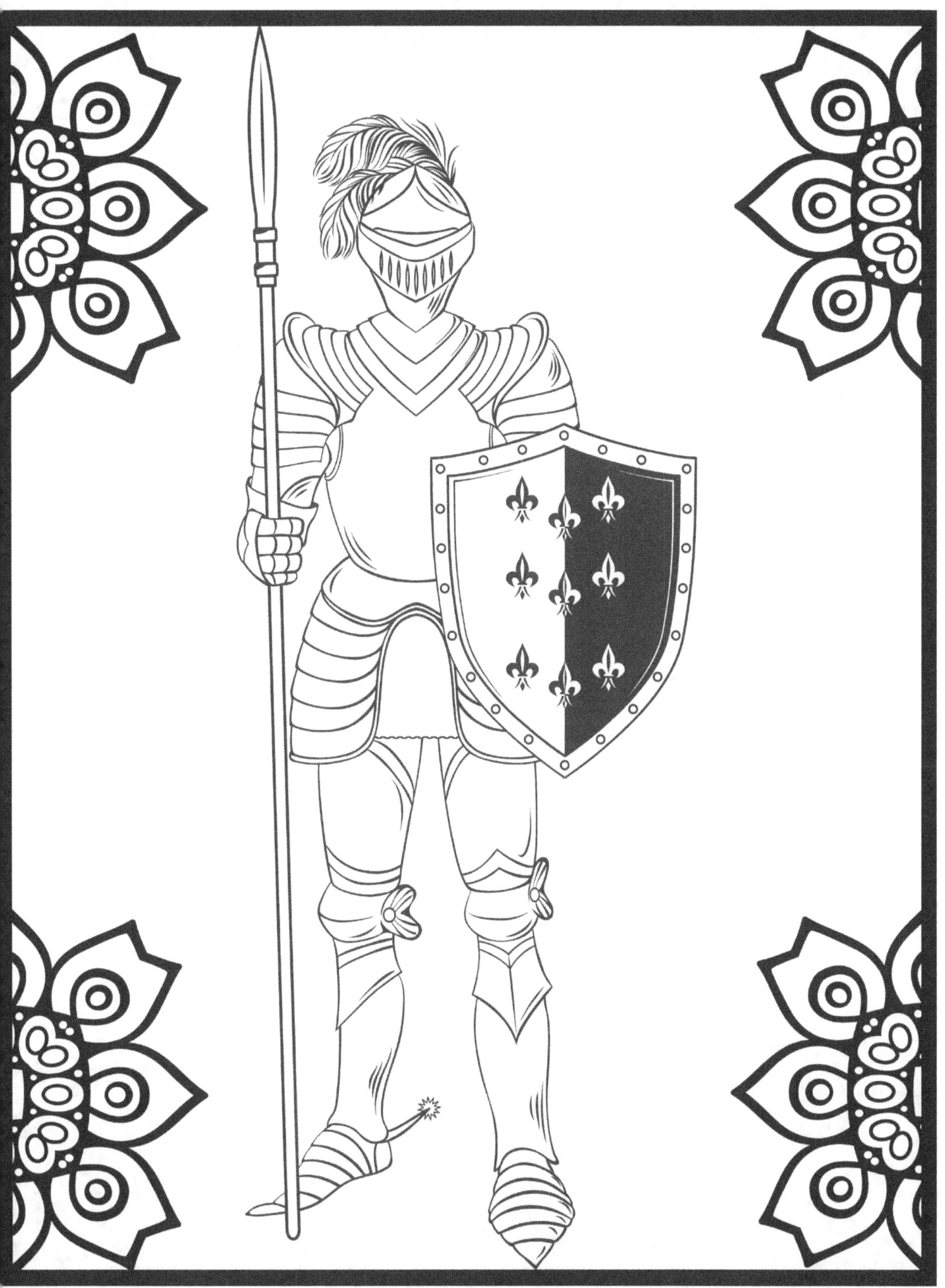

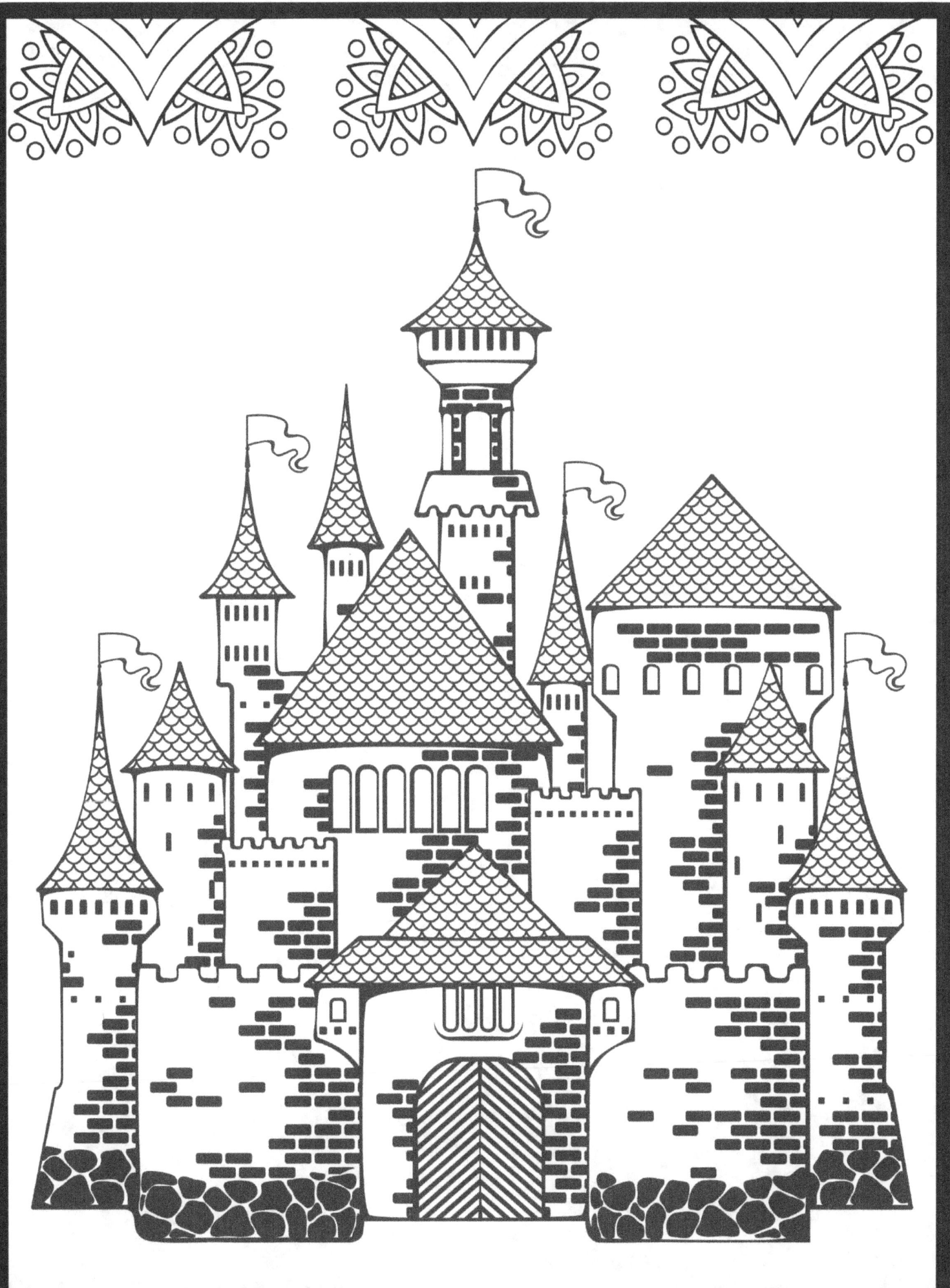

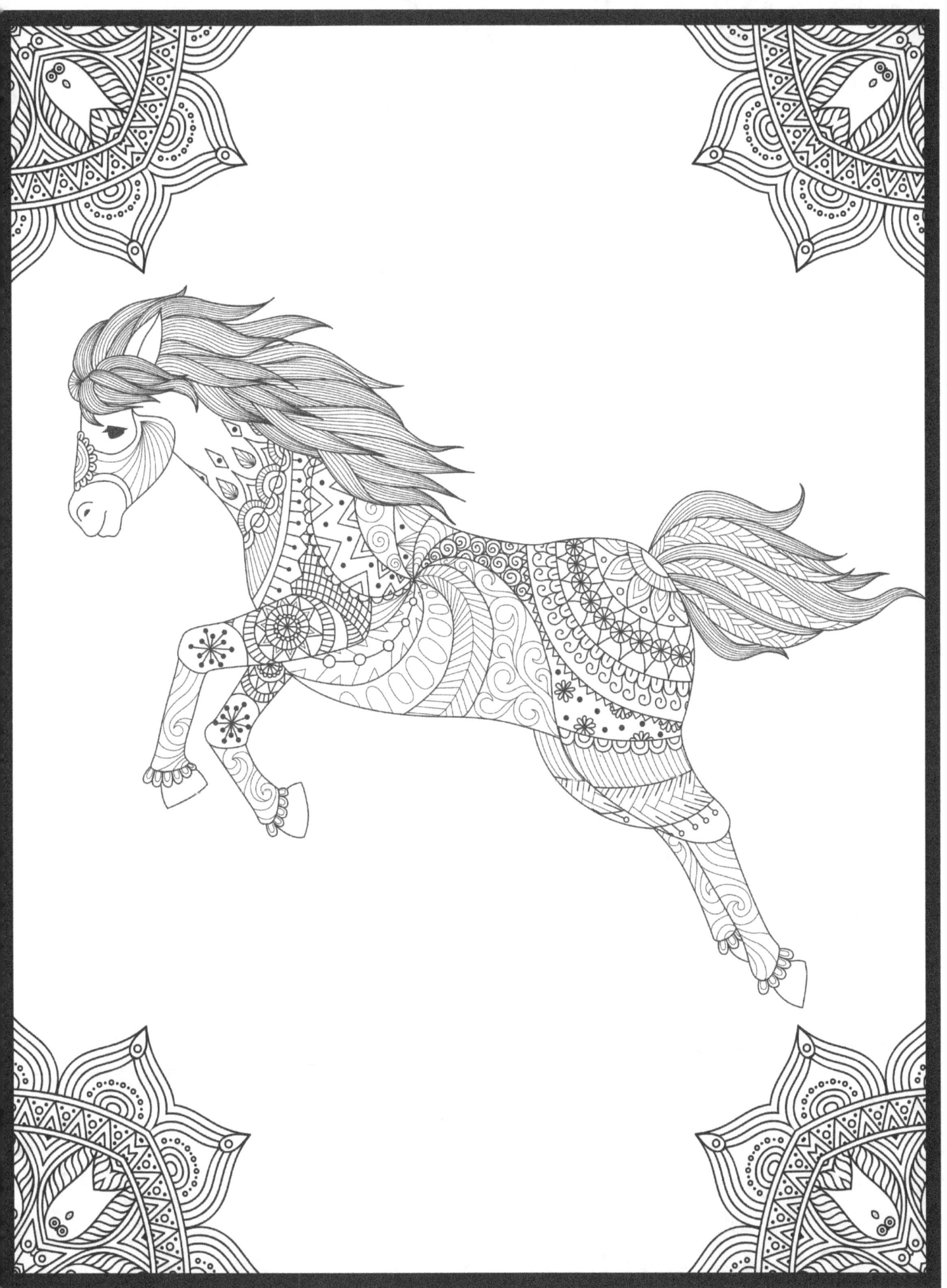

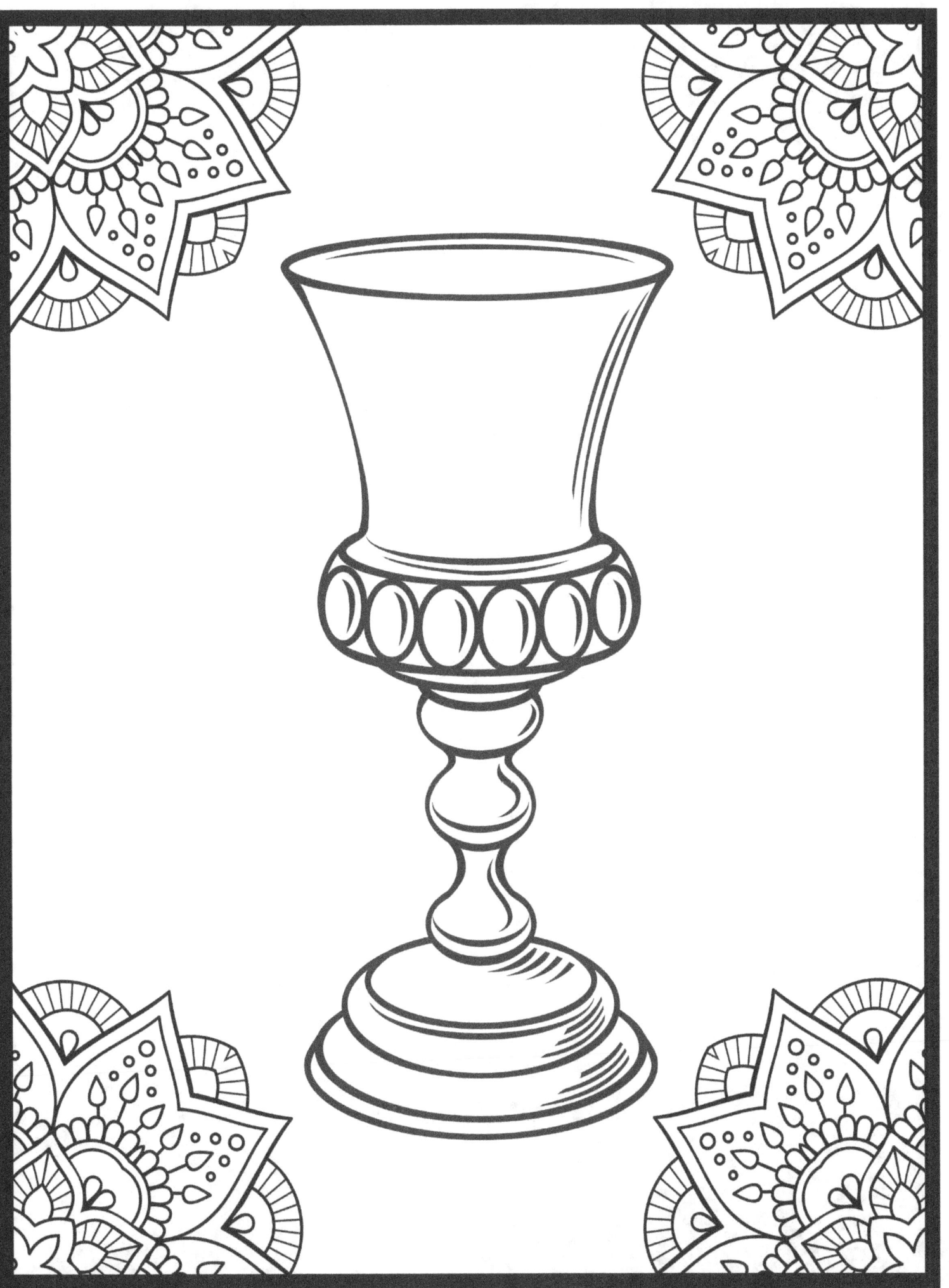

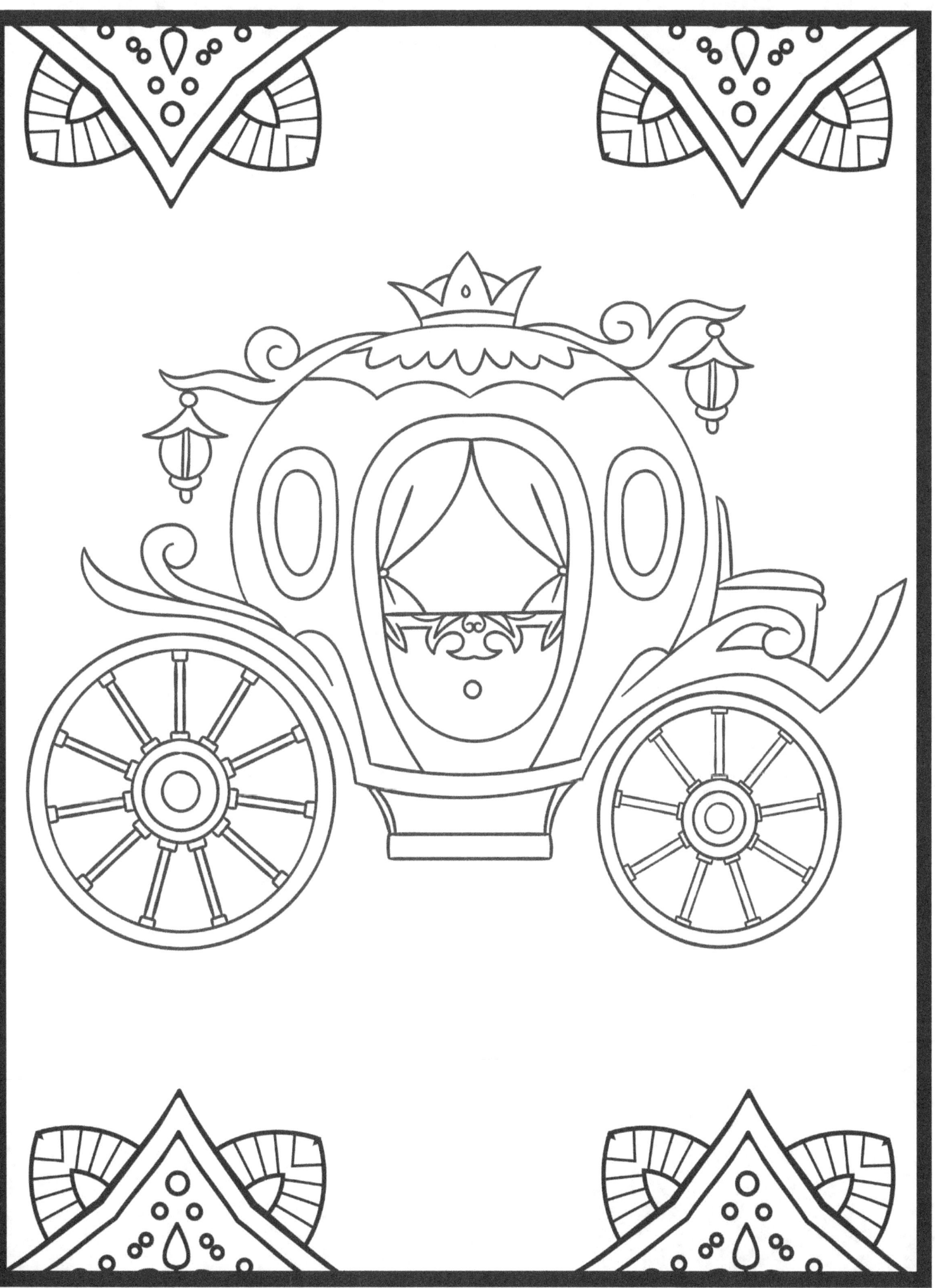

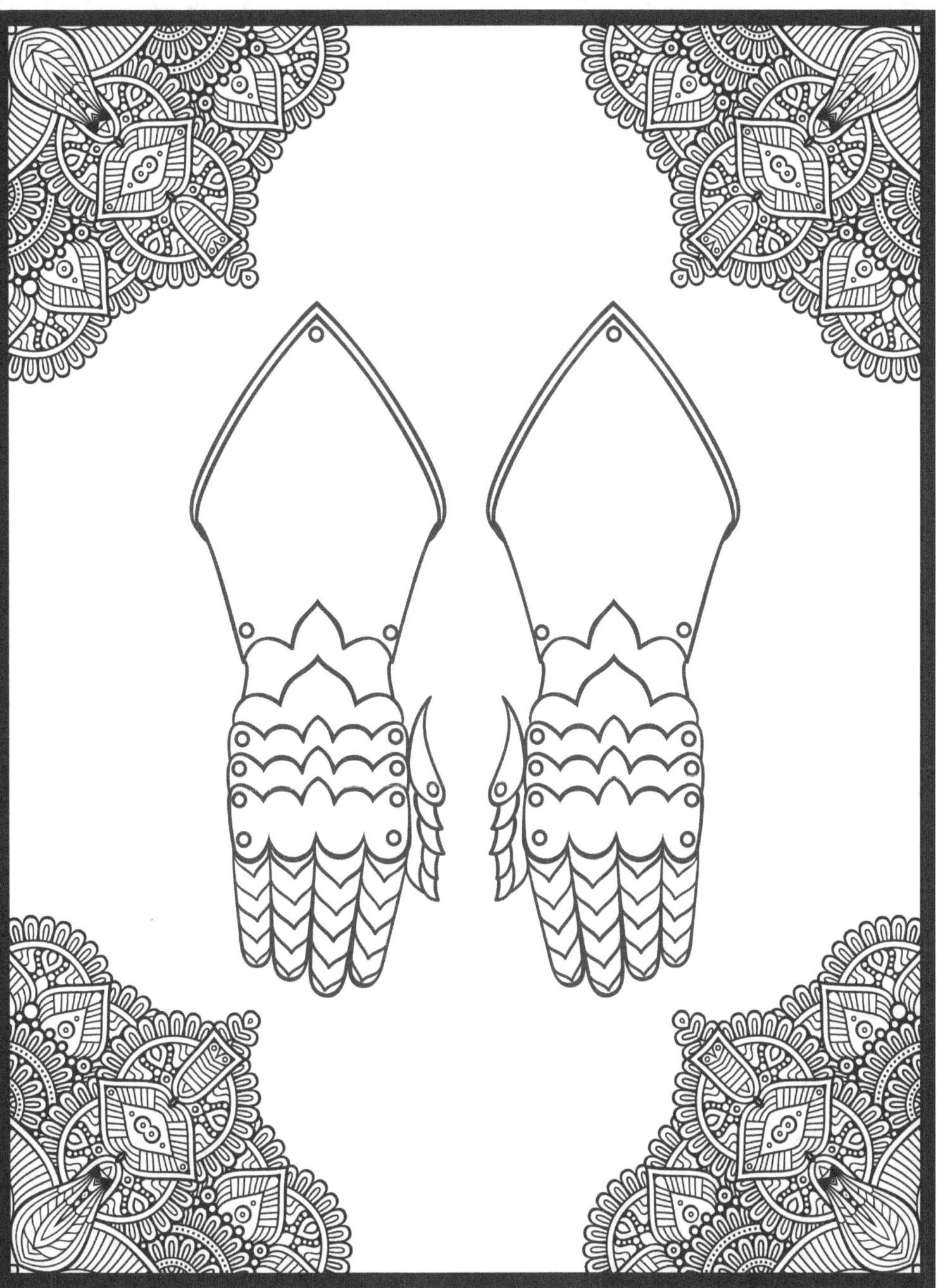

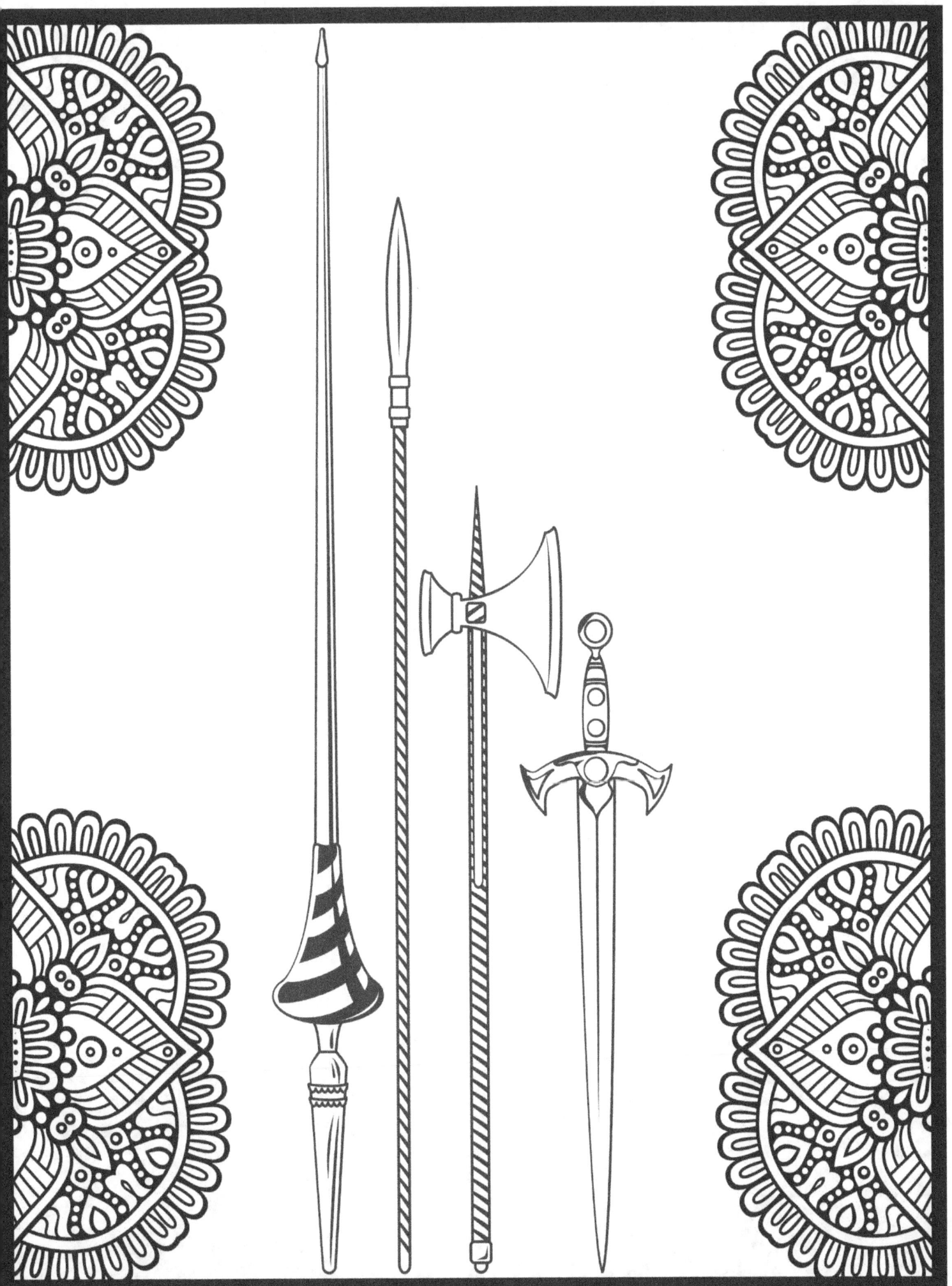

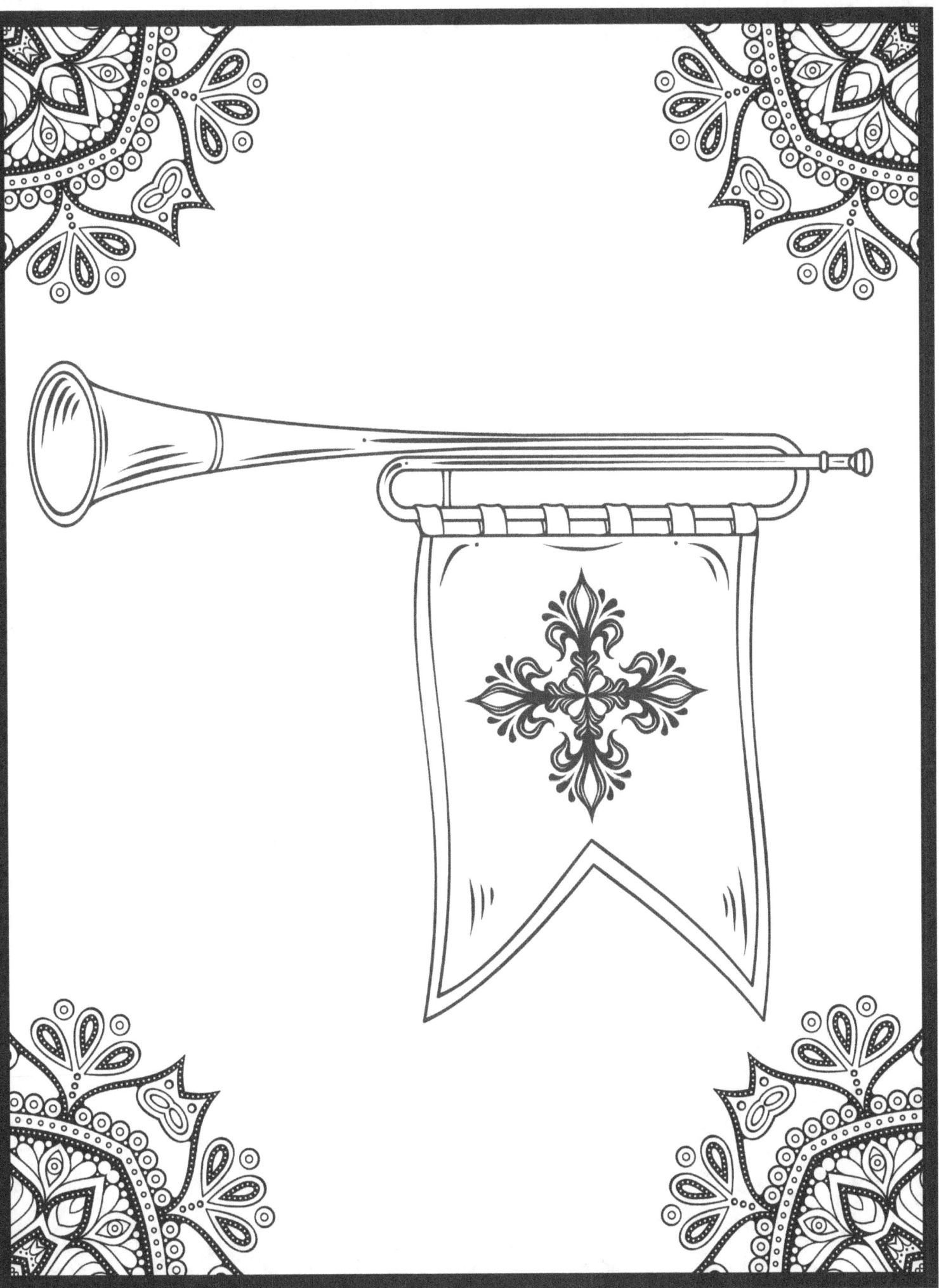

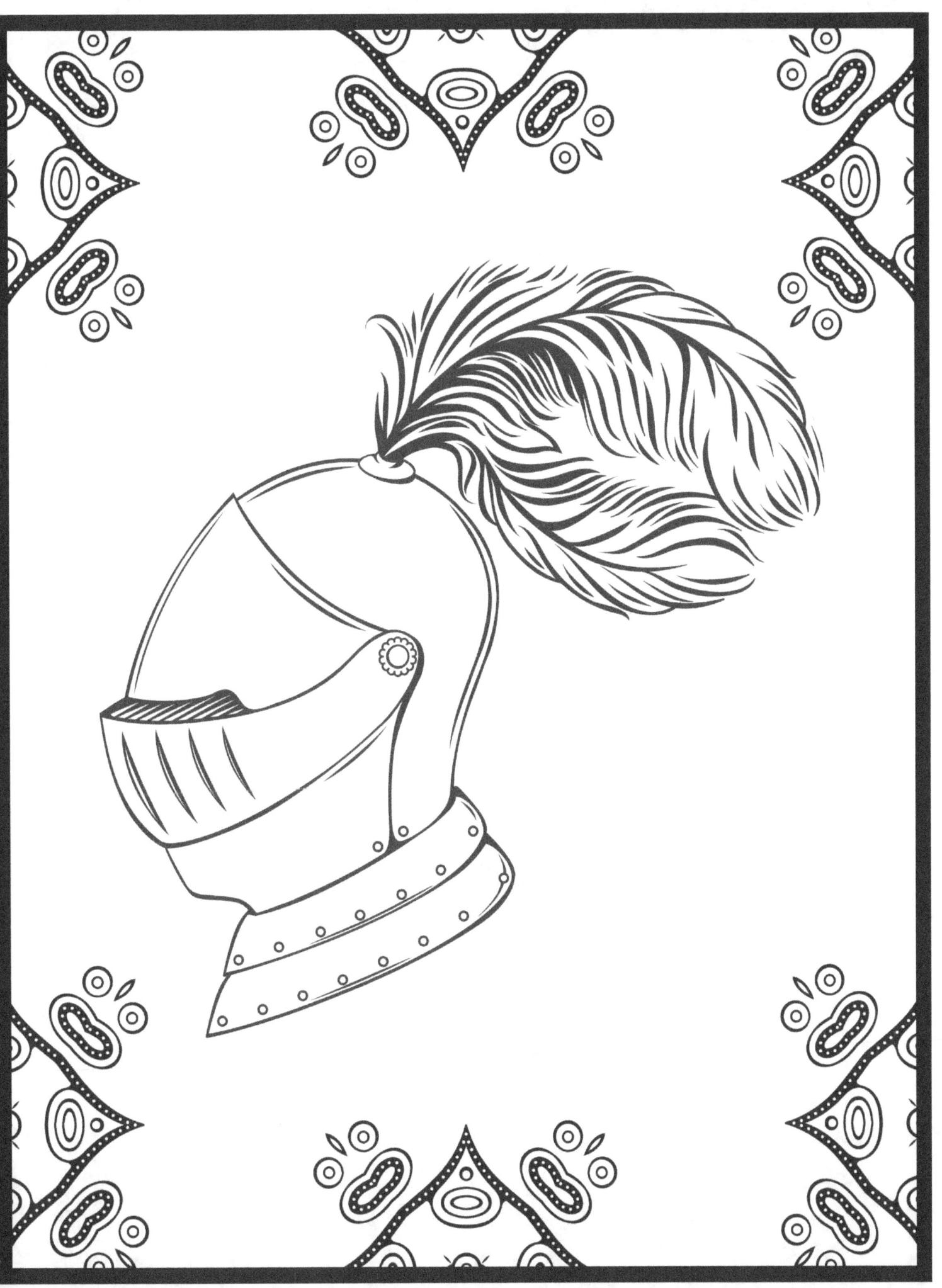

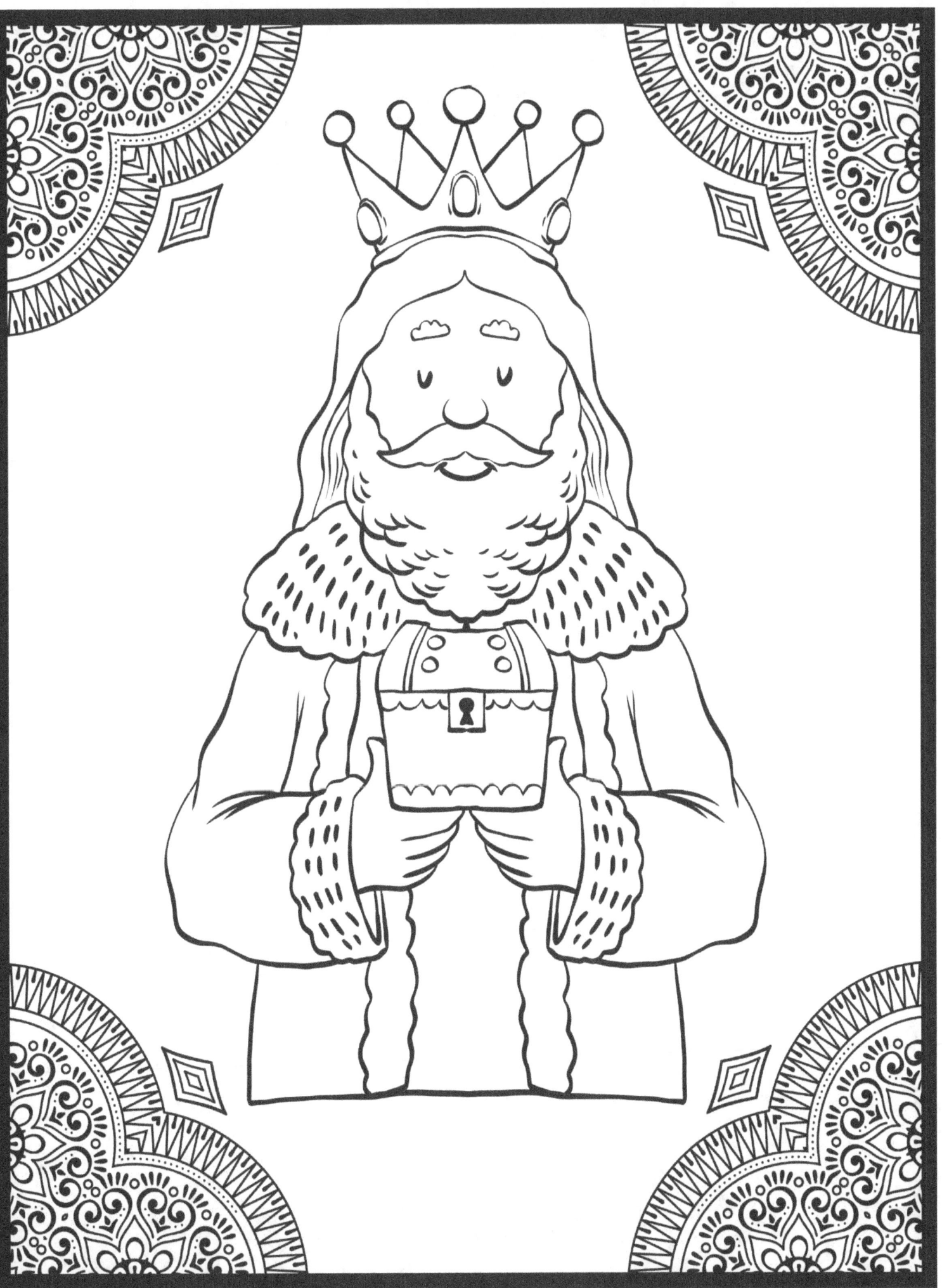

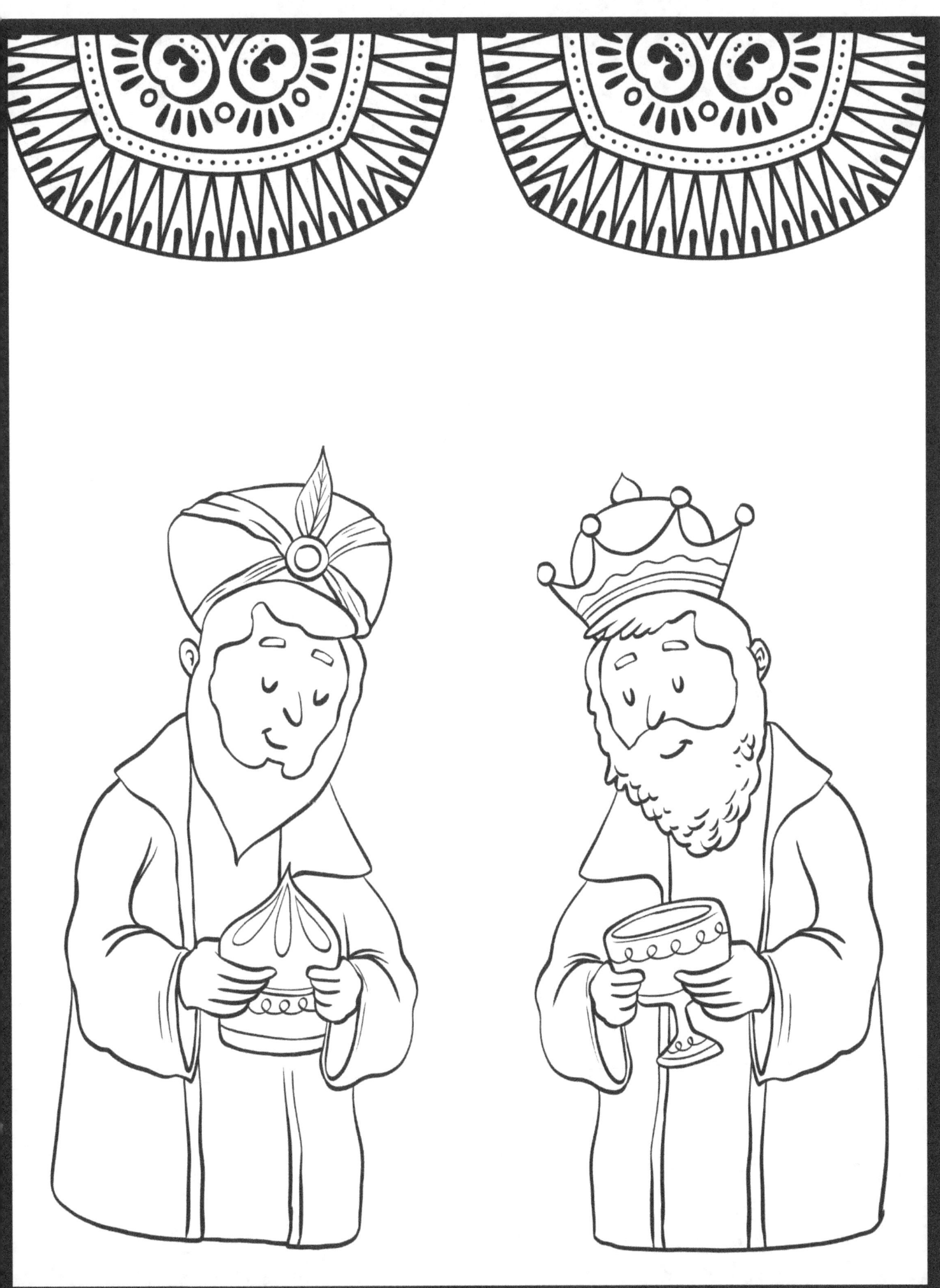

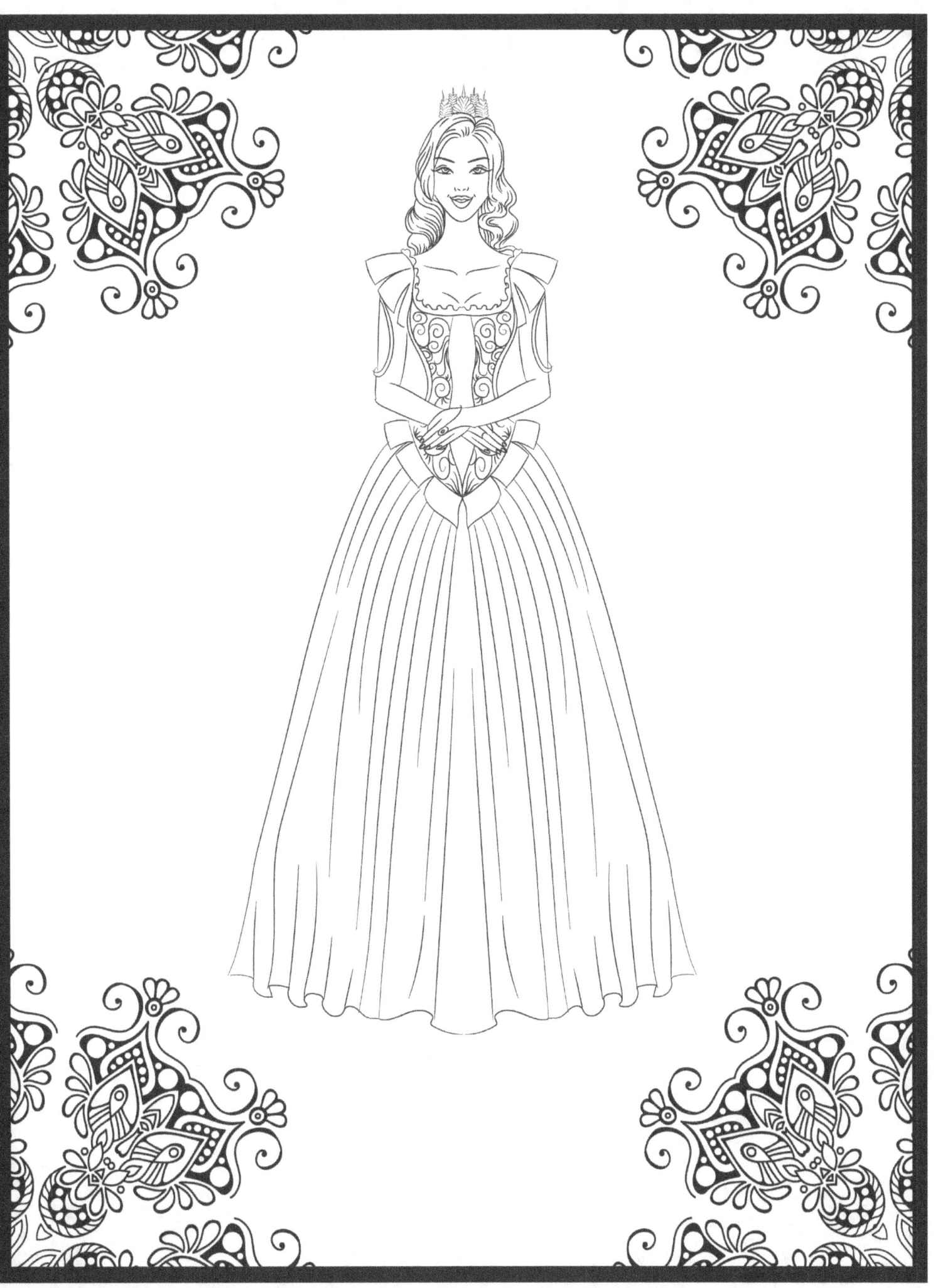

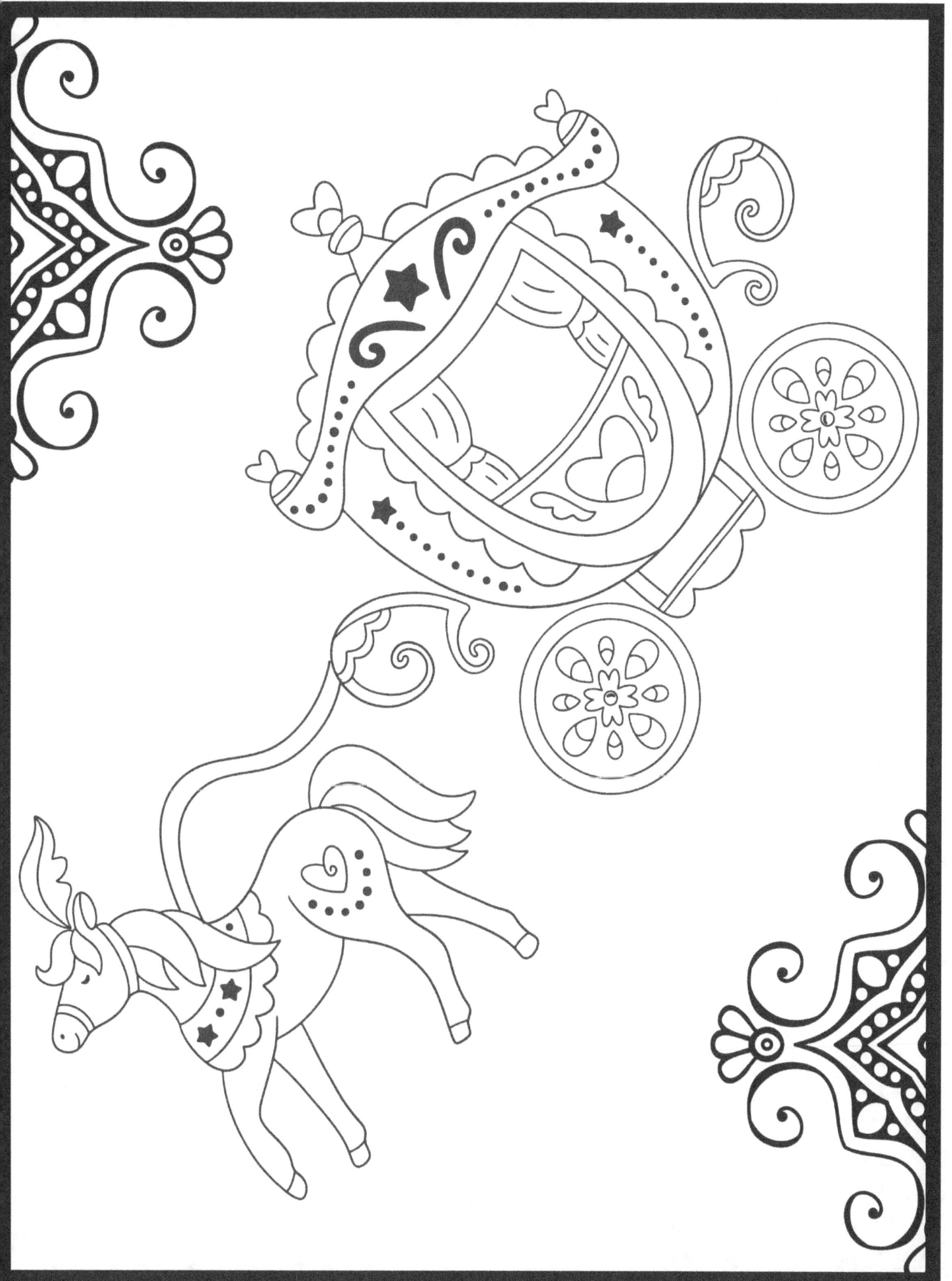

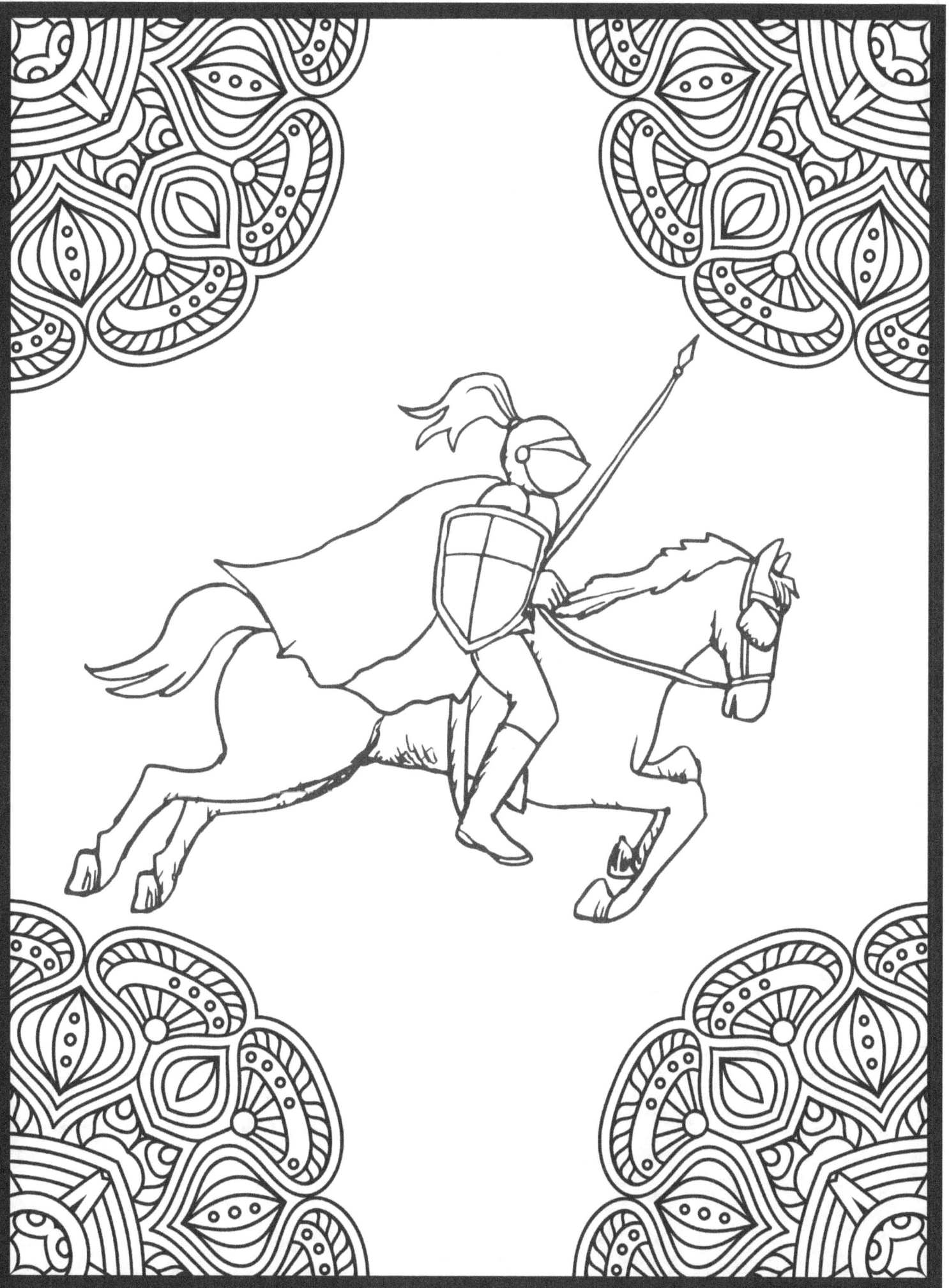

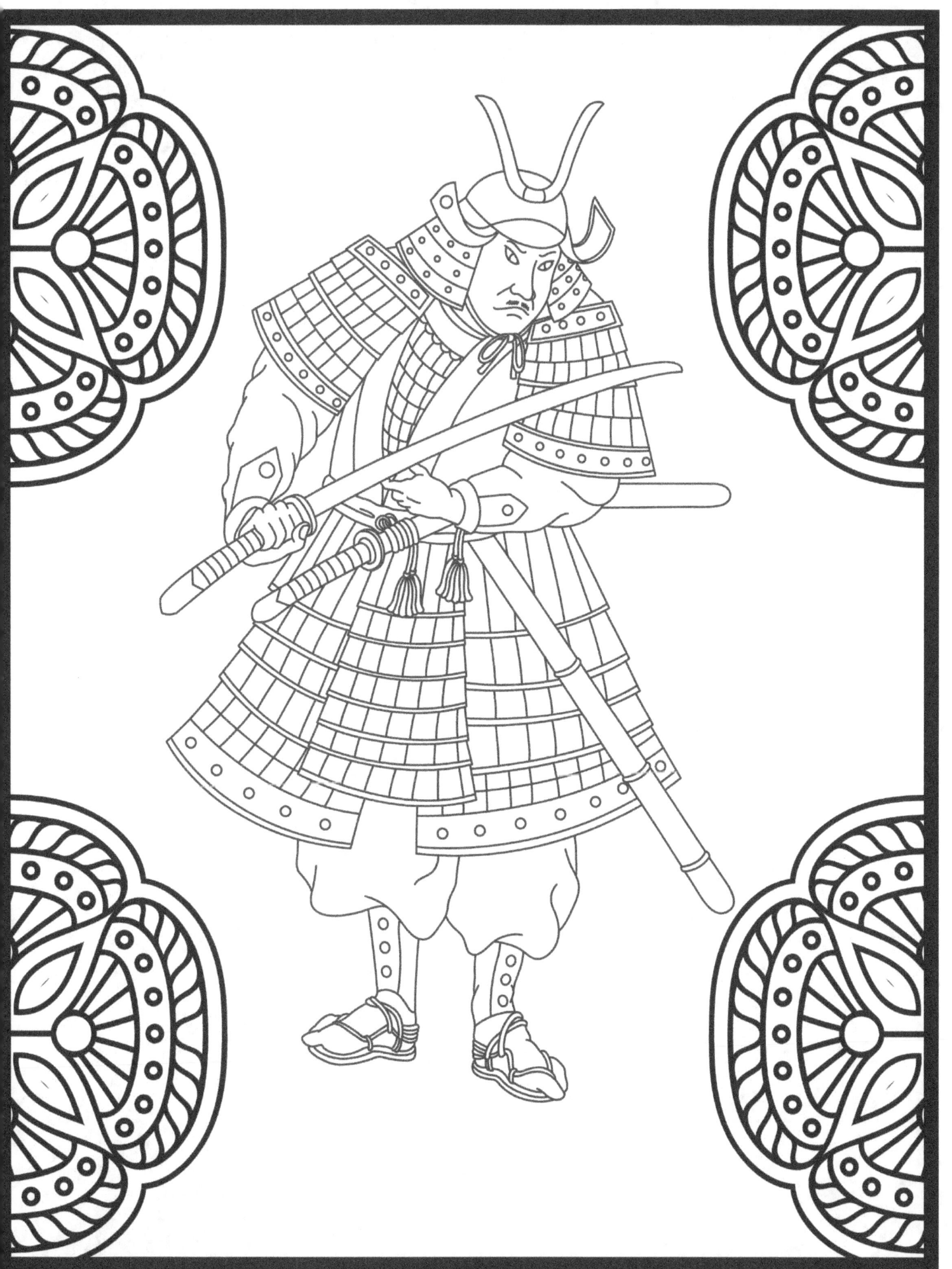

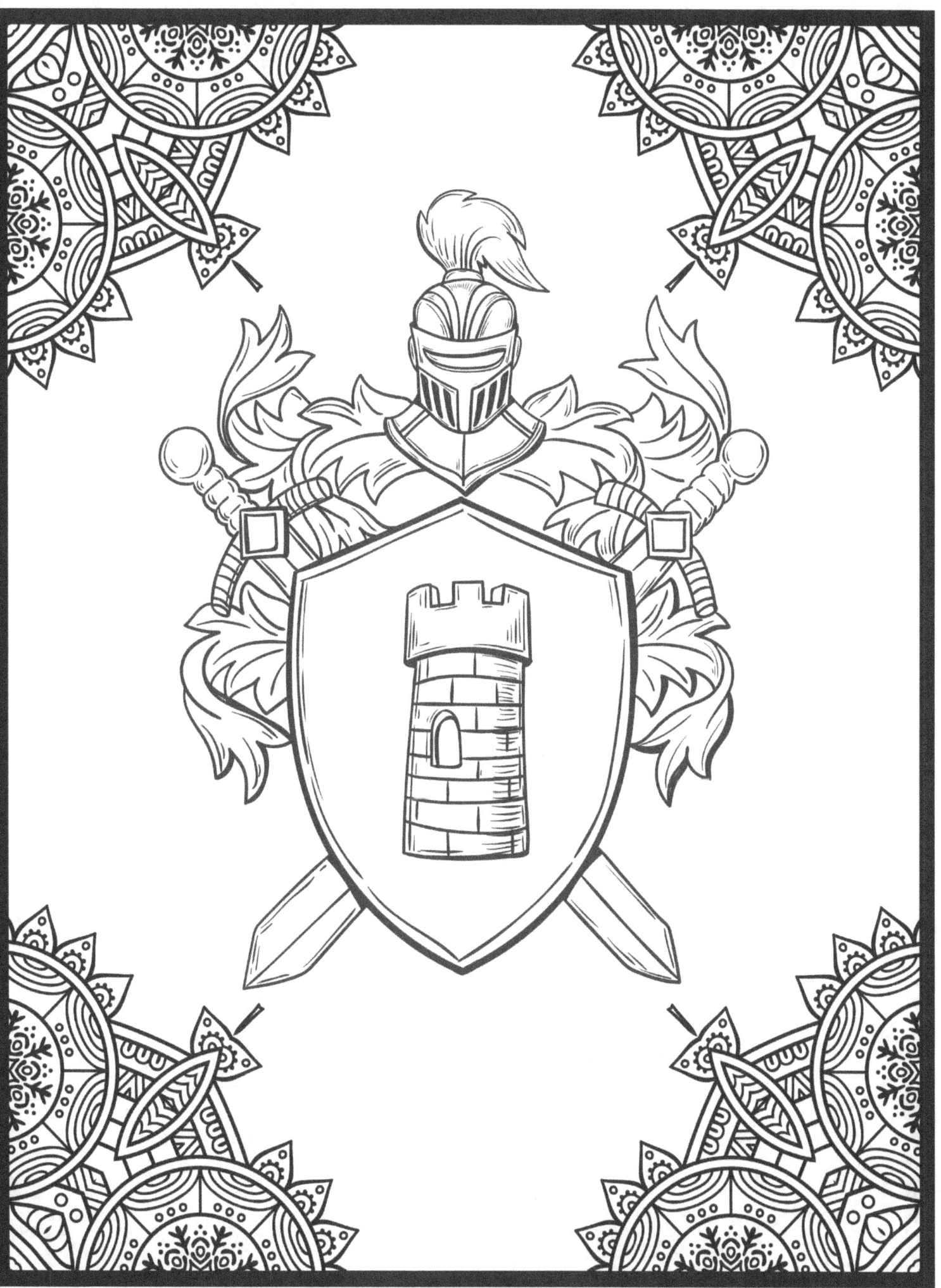

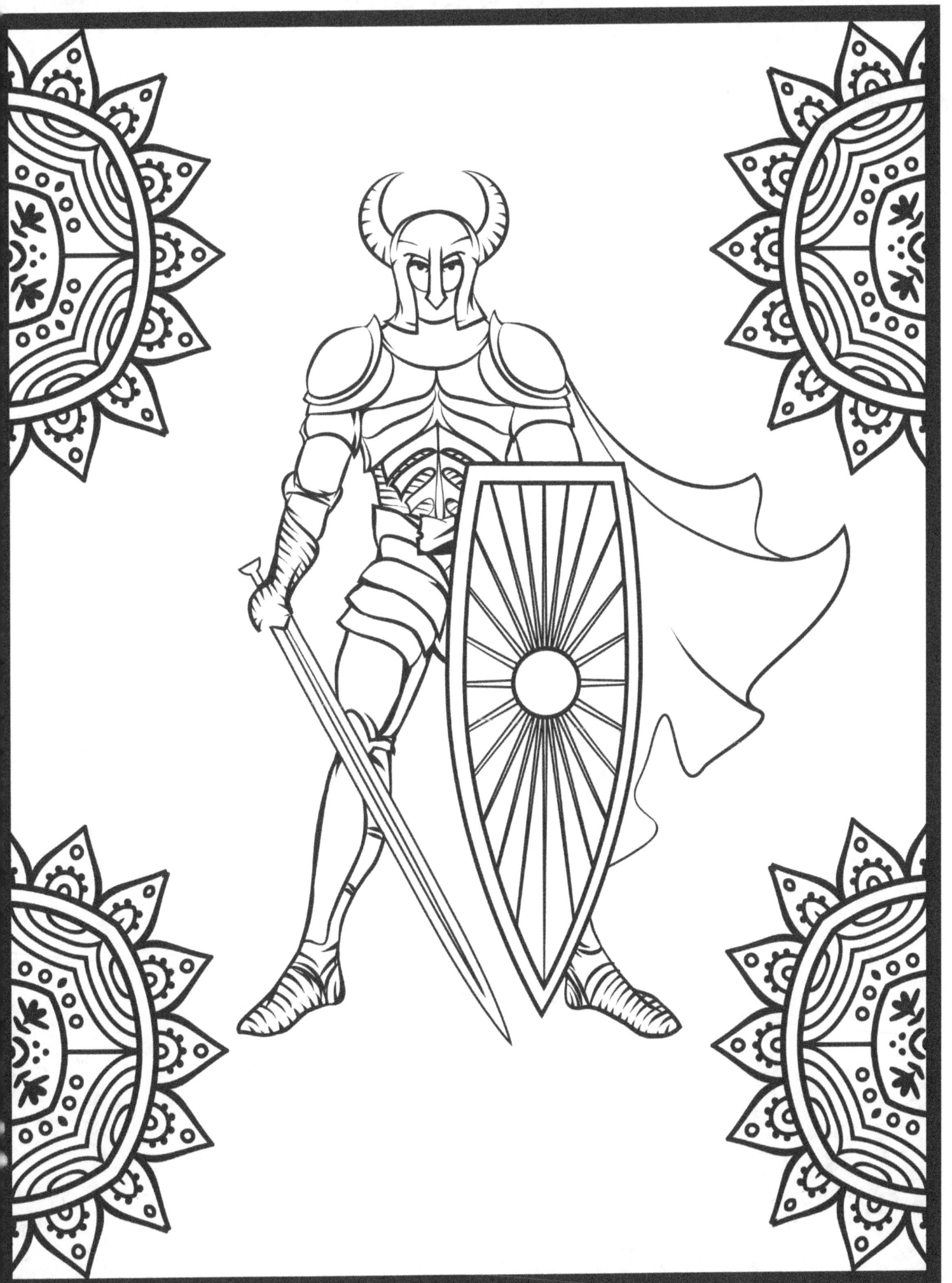

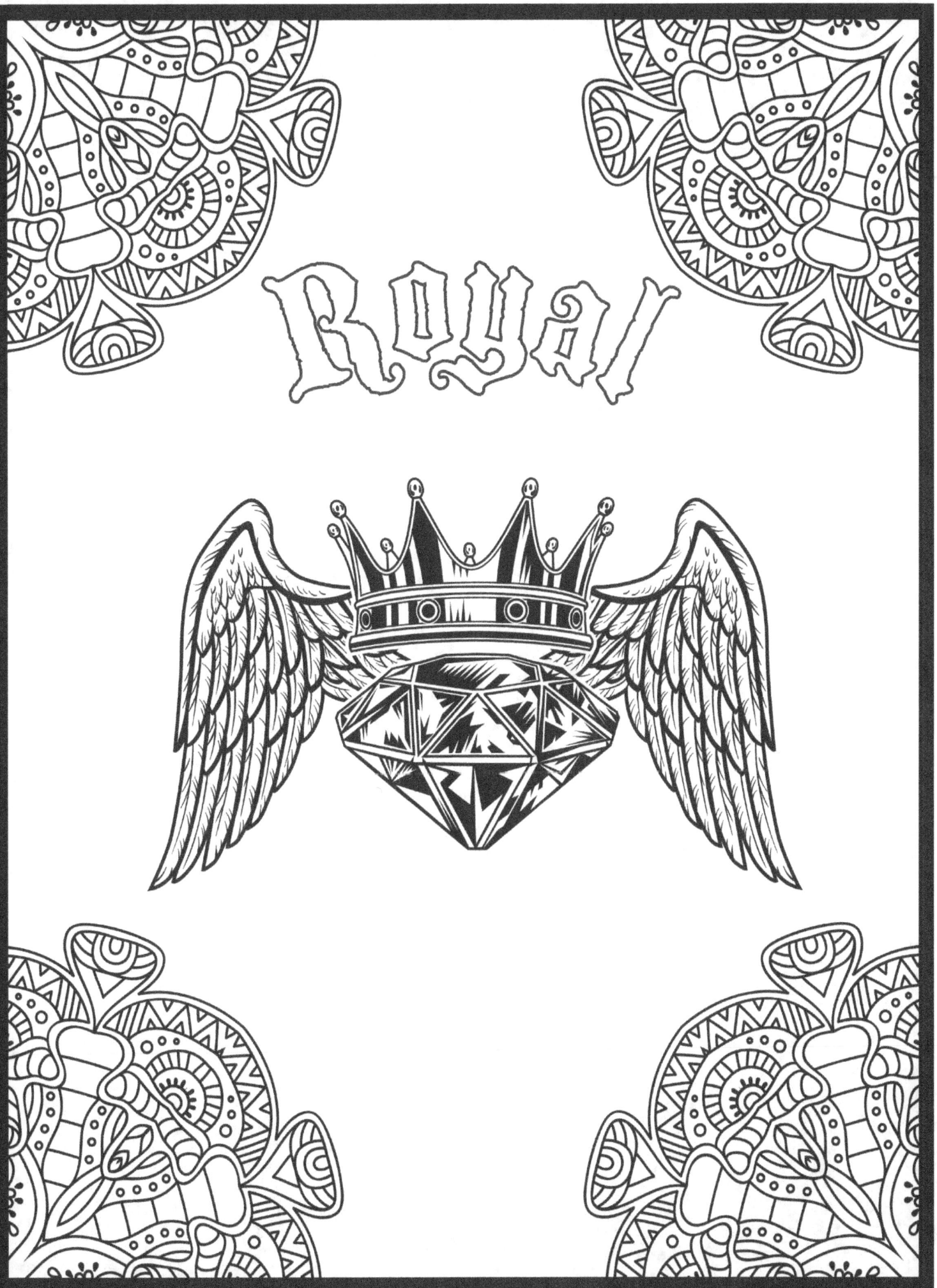

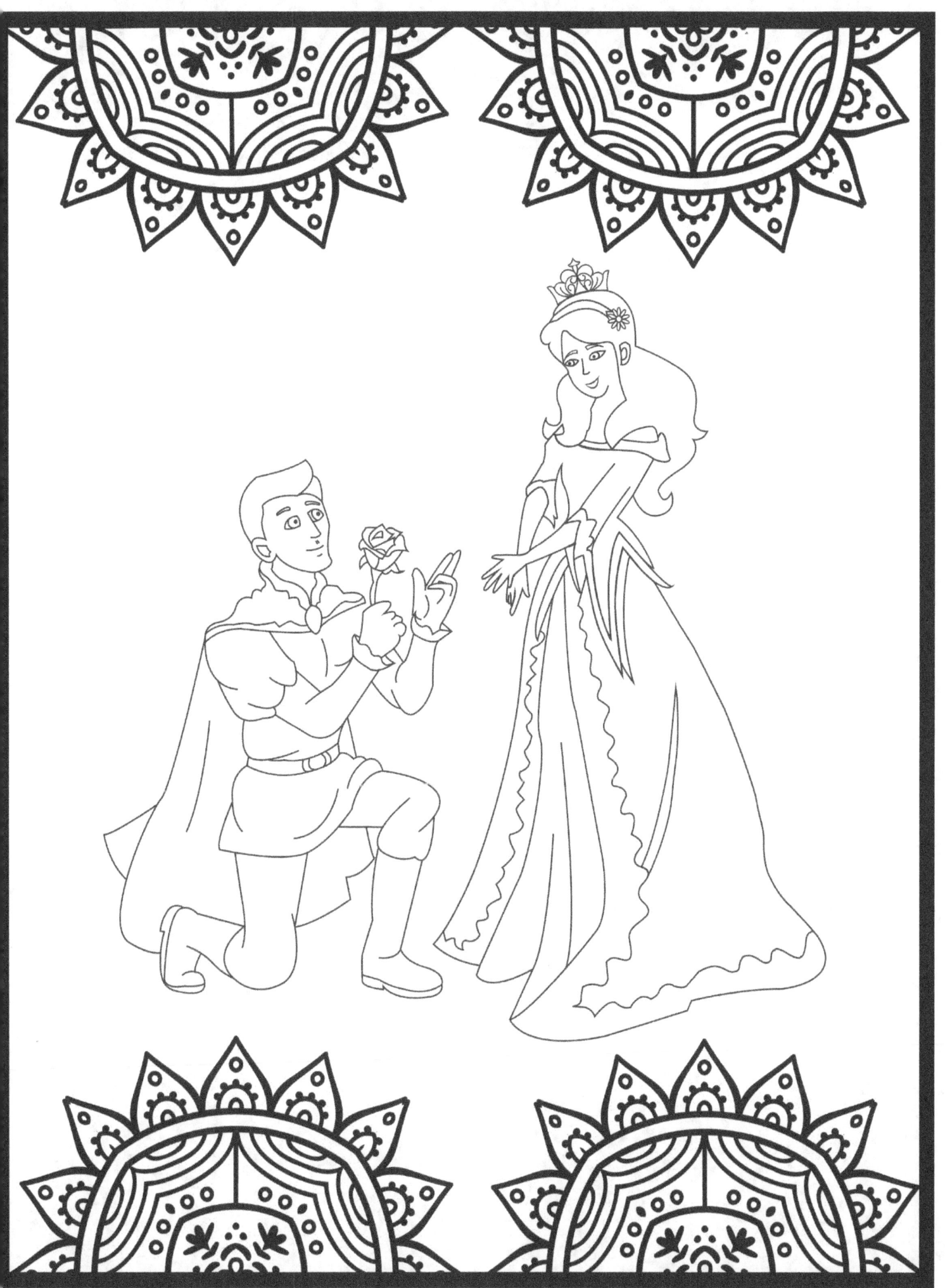

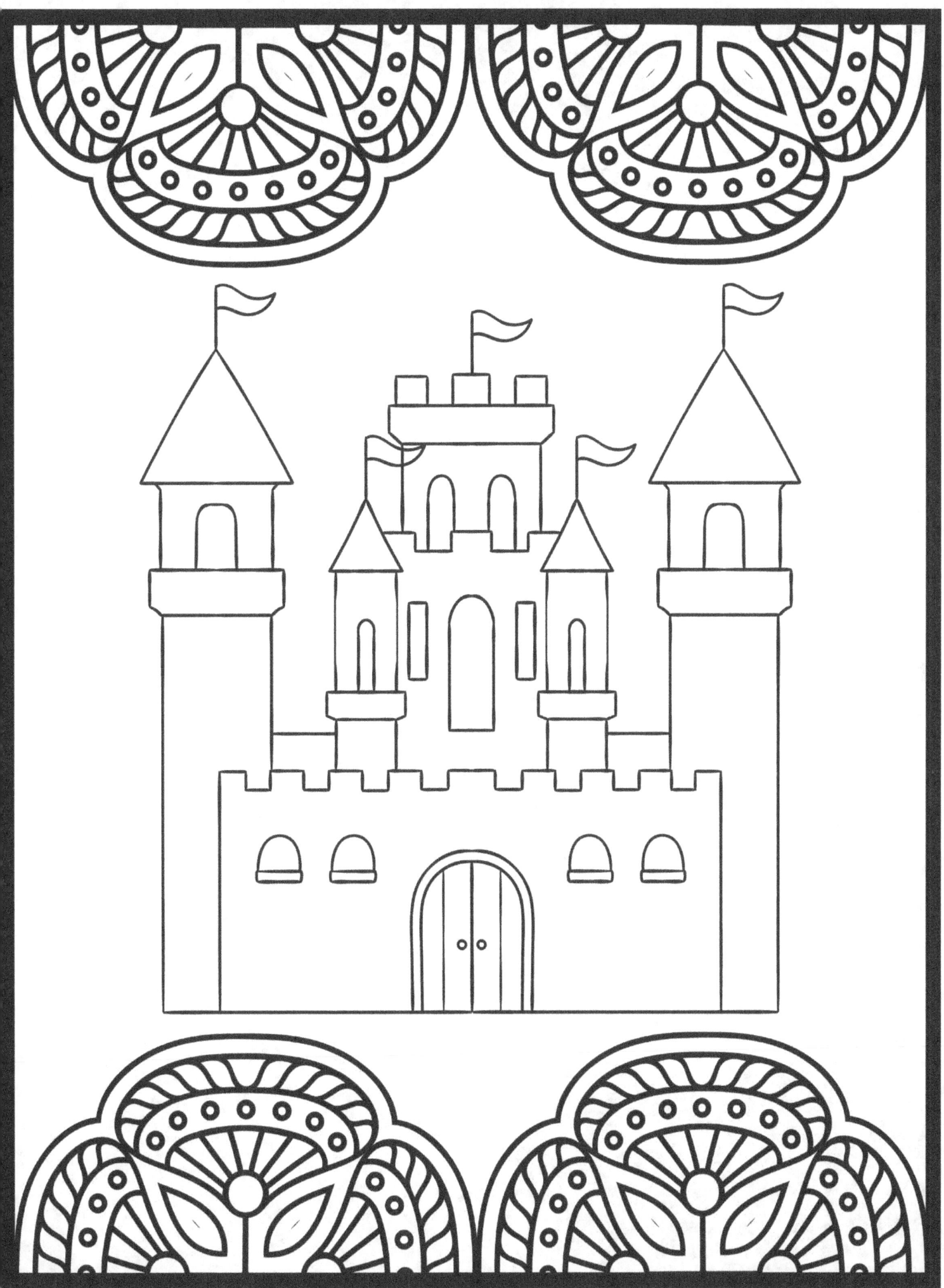

Other Coloring Books from Aryla Publishing

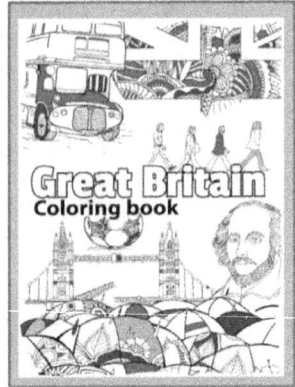
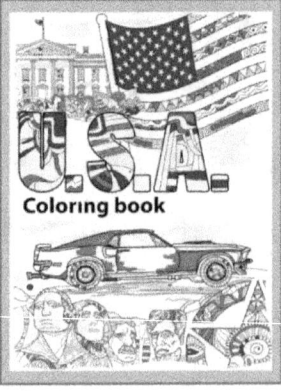
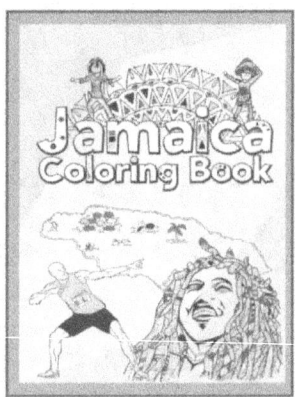
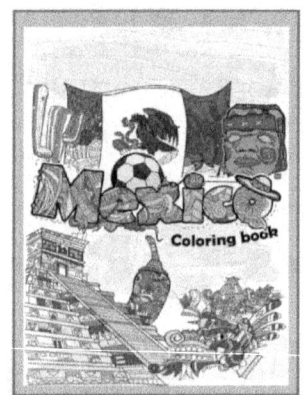

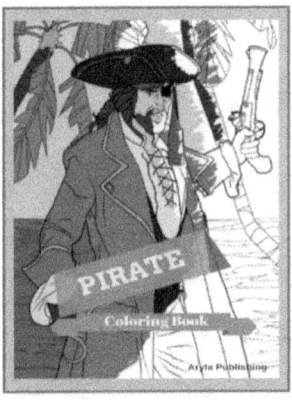
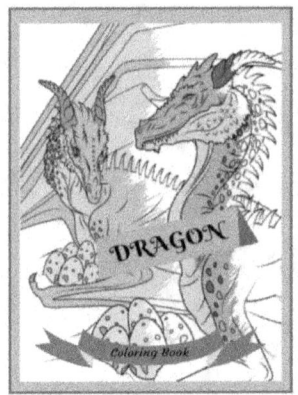
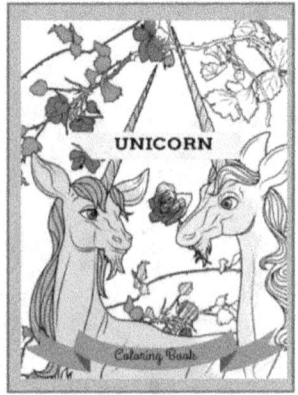
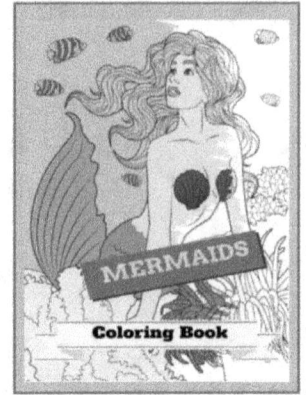

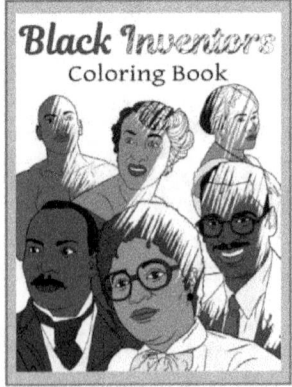
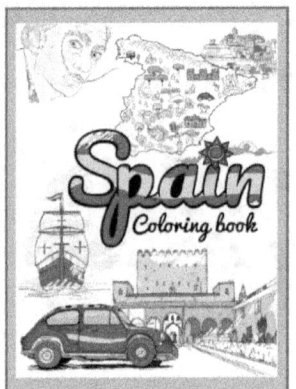
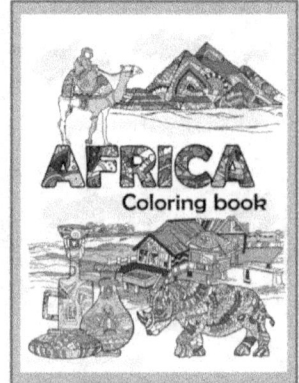
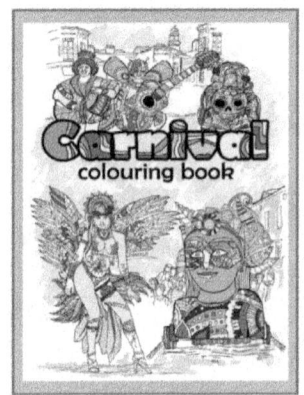

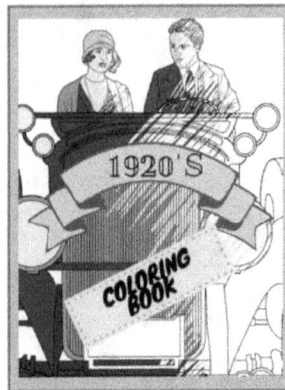
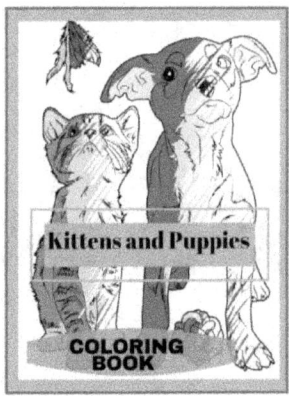
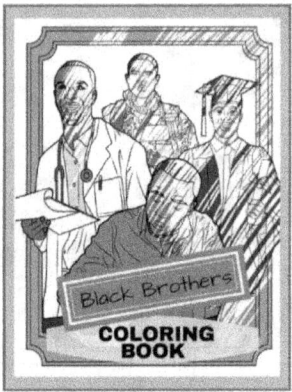
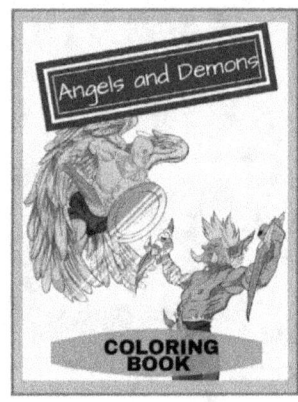

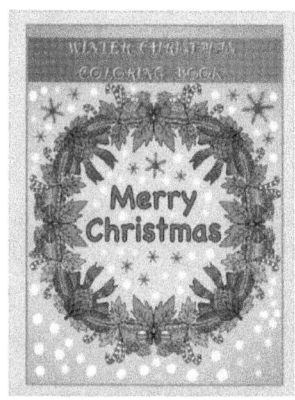
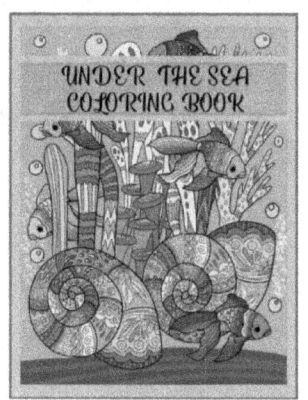
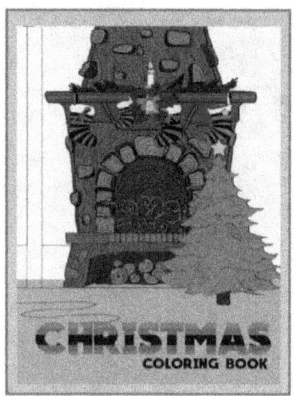
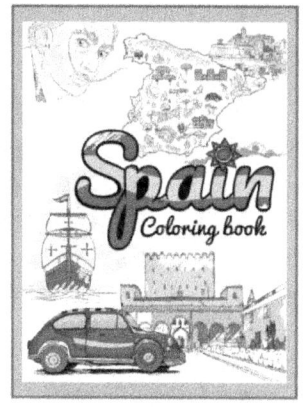
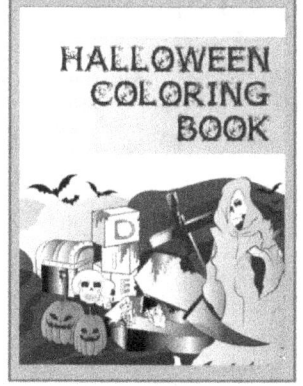
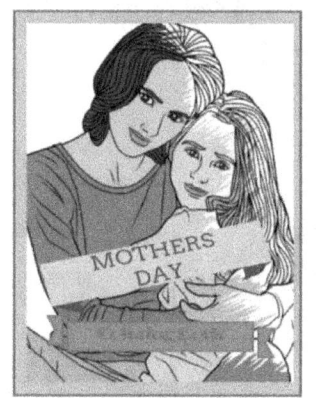
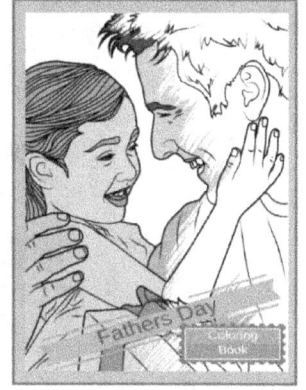
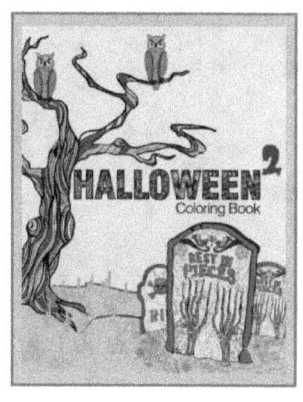
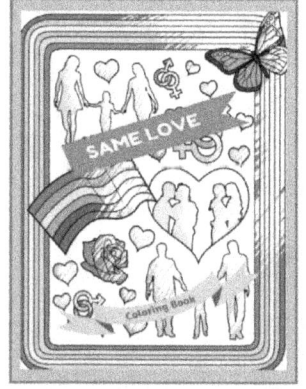
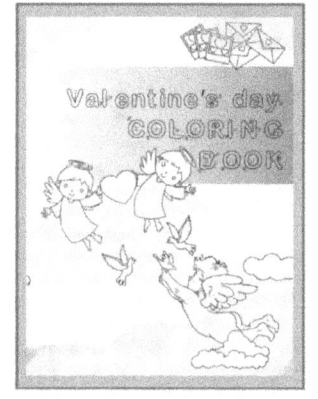
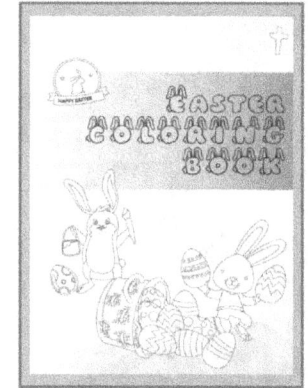
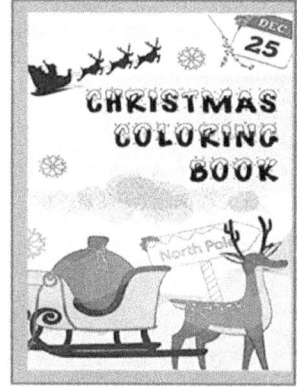
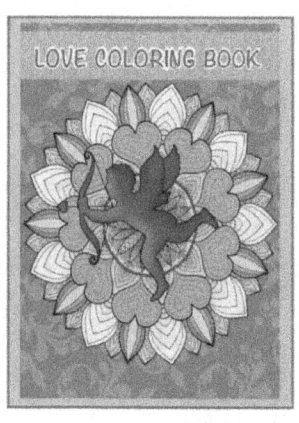
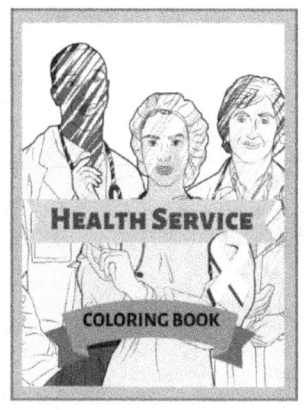
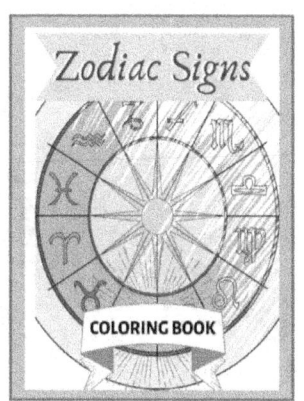
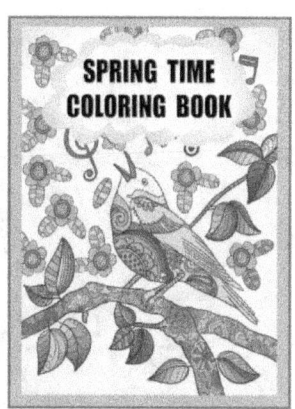

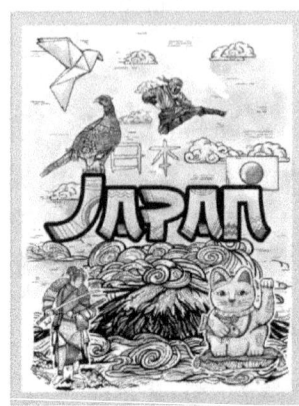

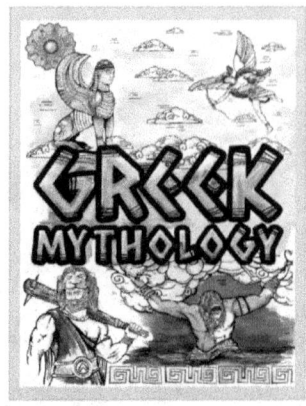

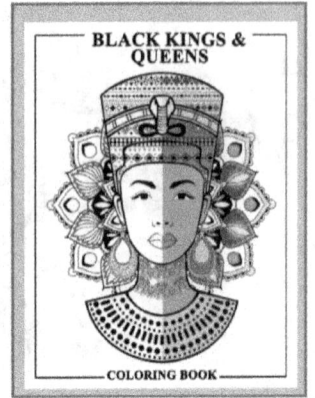

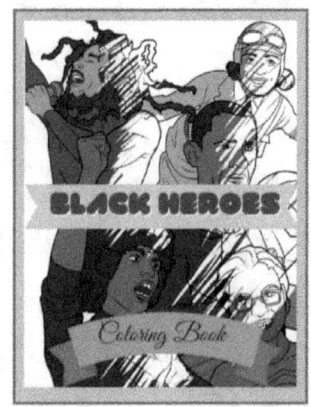

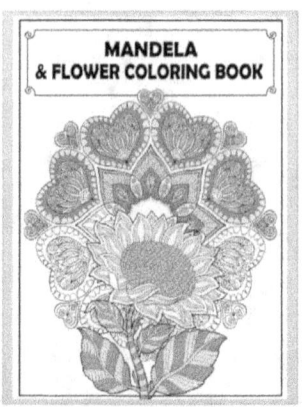

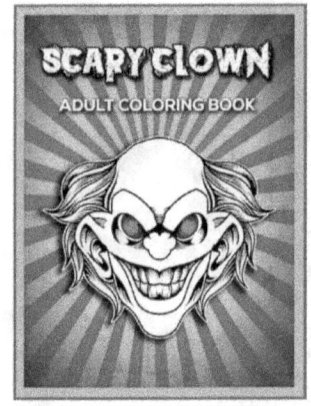

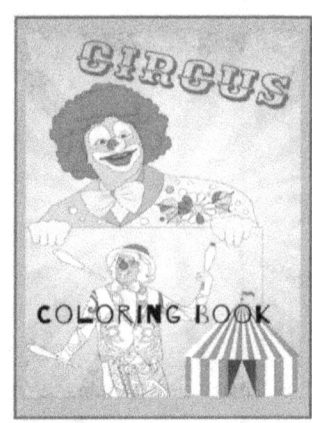

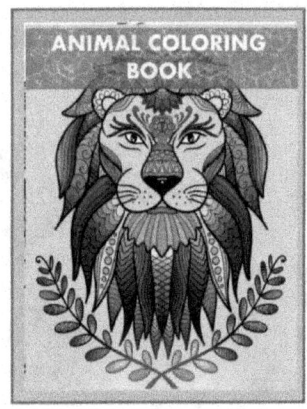

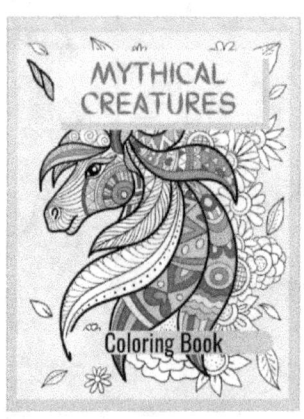

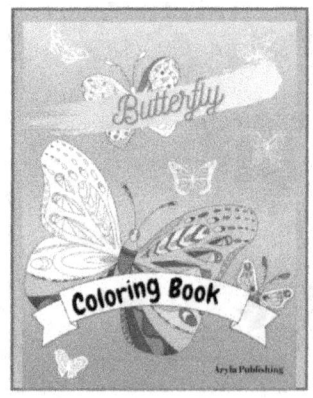

Color In Fun
Kids Books

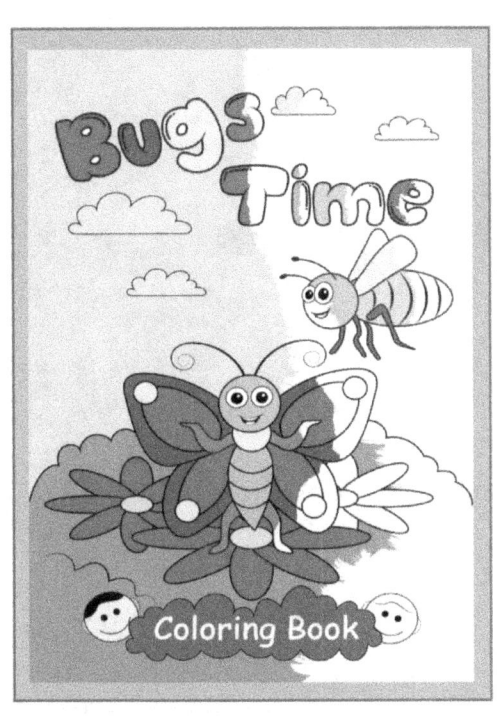

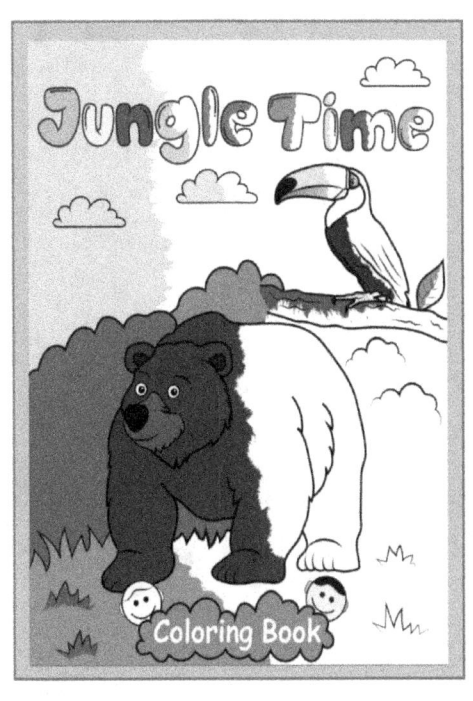

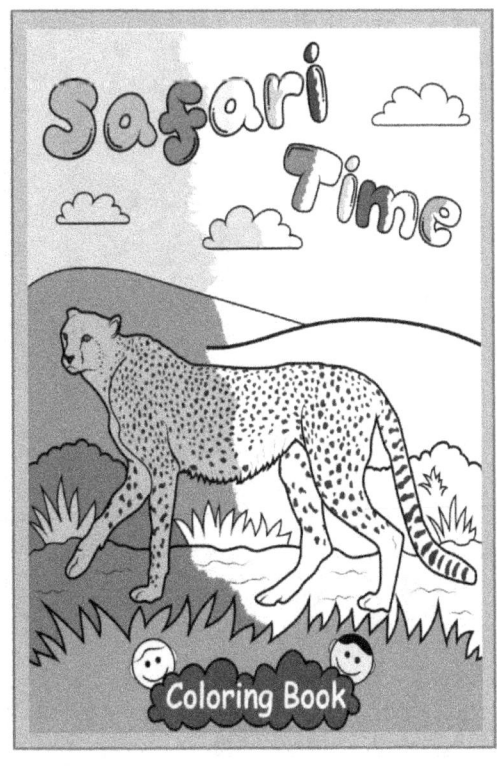

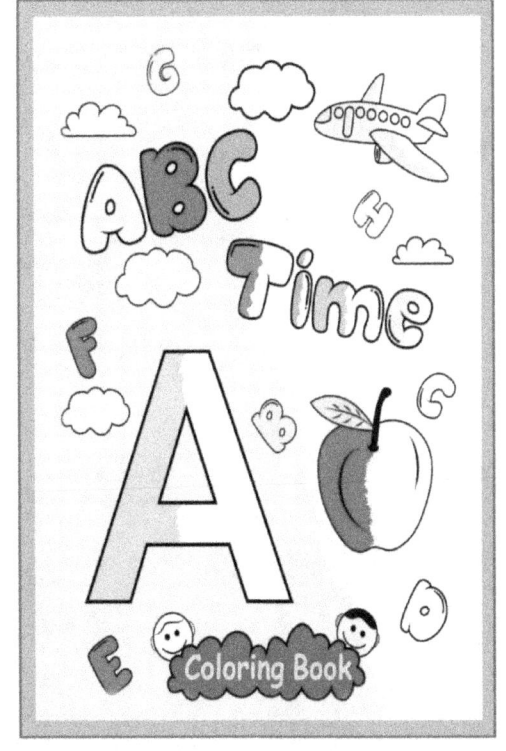

Visit **www.ArylaPublishing.com**
to find out about all new releases.

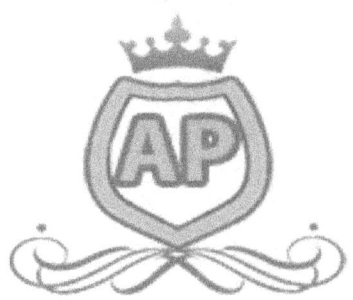

Follow us @arylapublishing on Twitter Instagram & Facebook

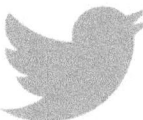  

Search for Aryla Publishing on

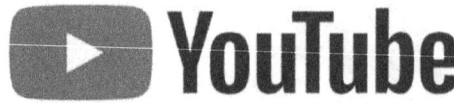 **YouTube**

Check out our <u>Book Trailers</u>

<u>Subscribe</u> **to keep up to date with new releases!**

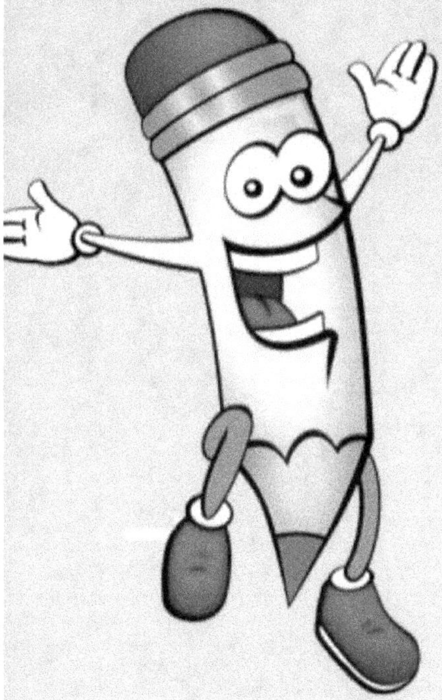

WE WOULD LOVE YOUR FEEDBACK

PLEASE LEAVE REVIEW AT:-